JE
BIBLE STUDY SERIES

JOHN

THE DIVINITY OF CHRIST

DR. DAVID JEREMIAH

Prepared by Hudson Bible

THOMAS NELSON
Since 1798

JOHN
JEREMIAH BIBLE STUDY SERIES

© 2019 by Dr. David Jeremiah

Published in Nashville, Tennessee, by Thomas Nelson. Thomas Nelson is a registered trademark of HarperCollins Christian Publishing, Inc.

Produced with the assistance of Hudson Bible (www.HudsonBible.com). Project staff include Christopher D. Hudson and Randy Southern.

All Scripture quotations are taken from The Holy Bible, New King James Version. Copyright © 1979, 1980, 1982 by Thomas Nelson. All rights reserved.

The quote by Clement in the Introduction is from Eusebius, *History of the Church*, 6:14. The quote by Irenaeus is from *Against Heresies*, 3:1.

Thomas Nelson titles may be purchased in bulk for educational, business, fundraising, or sales promotional use. For information, please e-mail SpecialMarkets@ThomasNelson.com.

ISBN 978-0-310-09155-4

First Printing April 2019 / Printed in the United States of America

CONTENTS

INTRODUCTION TO
The Gospel of John

"Jesus, walking by the Sea of Galilee, saw . . . Simon called Peter . . . [and] two other brothers, James the son of Zebedee, and John his brother . . . He called them, and immediately they left the boat and their father, and followed Him" (Matthew 4:18, 21–22). The Gospels state that Jesus called twelve men to be His disciples, but these three fishermen—Peter, James, and John— shared a special relationship with Him. They were given unique access to events such as the raising of Jairus's daughter (see Luke 8:49–51), the transfiguration (see Matthew 17:1–2), and Jesus' agony in the Garden of Gethsemane (see Mark 14:32–34). It is perhaps due to this special access that John's Gospel includes stories not found in the other Gospels, such as Jesus turning water into wine (see 2:1–12), His encounter with a Samaritan woman (see 4:1–42), and His raising of Lazarus from the dead (see 11:1–44). John's account thus gives us a unique glimpse from one of Jesus' closest disciples into the life, ministry, death, and resurrection of Christ.

AUTHOR AND DATE

The author of the Gospel of John only identifies himself as "the disciple whom Jesus loved." However, based on internal evidence within the manuscript, it is likely this disciple was a member of Jesus' inner circle—either Peter, James, or John. Since Peter makes reference to this beloved disciple (see 21:20), and because James was martyred early in the history of the church, the most likely candidate for the authorship falls to John. The early church fathers concurred with this assessment. Clement, who lived

c. AD 35–99, wrote, "John, perceiving that the external facts had been made plain in the Gospel, being urged by his friends, and inspired by the Spirit, composed a spiritual Gospel." Irenaeus (c. AD 130–202) noted, "John, the disciple of the Lord . . . did himself publish a Gospel." It is likely that John was the last of the four Gospels to be written, sometime between AD 80–90, from the city of Ephesus in Asia Minor.

BACKGROUND AND SETTING

The witness of the early church was that John was aware of the Synoptic Gospels of Matthew, Mark, and Luke. John thus wrote his narrative of Jesus' life to complement those Gospels and supply additional information to help readers understand the events depicted in those accounts. It is also possible that John, as he neared the end of his life, felt the need to record his personal recollections of Jesus' life and ministry in order to combat some of the false teachings that were beginning to circulate in the early church. But above all, John's intent was simply to lead people to find salvation in Christ. This is apparent from a statement he makes near the end of his account, where he states, "But these [words] are written that you may believe that Jesus is the Christ, the Son of God, and that believing you may have life in His name" (20:31).

KEY THEMES

Several key themes are prominent in John's Gospel. The first is that *Jesus was divine and existed before the creation of the world.* John begins his Gospel by stating, "In the beginning was the Word, and the Word was with God, and the Word was God" (1:1). John also repeatedly uses the phrase "Son of God" and "only begotten Son" throughout his Gospel to emphasize Jesus' divinity, and he records seven statements of Jesus that begin with "I am" (see 6:35; 8:12; 10:7–9; 10:11–14; 11:25; 14:6; 15:1–5). John's readers would have associated this identification with God's proclamation to Moses, when He said, "I AM WHO I AM" (Exodus 3:14).

A second theme is that *Jesus came to bring salvation to the world*. Early in John's Gospel, he records a conversation that Jesus had with a Pharisee named Nicodemus. At one point in the discussion, Jesus states that God sent Him into the world so "that whoever believes in Him should not perish but have everlasting life" (3:16). John captures many other instances of Jesus using the word *life* in His teaching, offering those who believe in Him the bread of life, water of life, abundant life, and the way to life (see 6:33; 7:37–38; 10:10; 14:6).

A third theme is that *Jesus demonstrated the arrival of God's kingdom through signs*. John constructed his account of Jesus' ministry around seven key miracles to reveal how Jesus, as the Son of God, had the power to turn water into wine (2:1–11), heal an official's son (4:46–54), heal a sick man at Bethesda (5:1–15), feed more than 5,000 people (6:5–13), walk on water (6:16–21), heal a blind man (9:1–7), and even raise Lazarus from the dead (11:1–44). John also uses terms such as *life* and *death*, *light* and *darkness*, and *love* and *hate* to contrast His life-giving ministry against the works of Satan, who only seeks " to kill, and to destroy" (10:10).

A fourth theme is that *Jesus called His followers to continue His mission*. John relates a story at the end of his Gospel in which the resurrected Jesus miraculously appeared to His disciples as they were gathered together in a home. Jesus greeted them, showed them His pierced hands and side, and then said, "As the Father has sent Me, I also send you" (20:21). Jesus' commission to His disciples still applies to His followers today. Just as the Father sent Jesus to share the gospel with the world, so the Father sends us into the world to do the same.

KEY APPLICATIONS

John reveals how Jesus came to provide "living water" to quench our deep *spiritual thirst* for the things of God (7:38). He shows how Jesus is the "bread of life" who satisfies our deep *spiritual hunger* (6:35). And he reveals how Jesus is the *only way* we can obtain that living water and bread of life, for "no one comes to the Father" except through Him (14:6).

IN THE BEGINNING

John 1:1–2:25

GETTING STARTED

What are some of your fondest memories of meeting someone you respected?

_____

_____

_____

_____

_____

_____

_____

_____

_____

_____

_____

_____

_____

_____

_____

_____

_____

_____

SETTING THE STAGE

The apostle John used *Word* as a synonym for Jesus Christ. The word, translated from the Greek word *logos*, was used to define what Greek philosophers called the fundamental principle behind the way the universe functioned. John knew his readers would be familiar with *logos*, so he chose that word to communicate who Jesus Christ is. Not only is He the fundamental principle of the universe, but He is also the communication of God to man.

Jesus is the idea, the expression, and the manifestation of God to the whole world. He is God's Word to humankind. God in heaven, wanting to best communicate in a way we could understand, decided that He would come to earth in a human body to live among humans. Thus the God-man, Jesus Christ, was the Word of God to us.

Certainly, an idea can be cold and passionless, without any meaning. But it is different when that idea reaches out and takes hold of your hand. It's different when that idea walks, talks, breathes, and speaks among you. It's different when you can watch Him, feel Him, touch Him, hear Him, and be a part of His life. When that happens, an idea explodes into meaning so you can understand what the idea is all about.

We could not have known God as we do today had it not been for His Word. That Word, Jesus Christ, was—and is—God's Word to us.

EXPLORING THE TEXT

The Eternal Word (John 1:1–18)

> ¹ In the beginning was the Word, and the Word was with God, and the Word was God. ² He was in the beginning with God. ³ All things were made through Him, and without Him nothing was made that was made. ⁴ In Him was life, and the life was the light of men. ⁵ And the light shines in the darkness, and the darkness did not comprehend it.

⁶ There was a man sent from God, whose name was John. ⁷ This man came for a witness, to bear witness of the Light, that all through him might believe. ⁸ He was not that Light, but was sent to bear witness of that Light. ⁹ That was the true Light which gives light to every man coming into the world.

¹⁰ He was in the world, and the world was made through Him, and the world did not know Him. ¹¹ He came to His own, and His own did not receive Him. ¹² But as many as received Him, to them He gave the right to become children of God, to those who believe in His name: ¹³ who were born, not of blood, nor of the will of the flesh, nor of the will of man, but of God.

¹⁴ And the Word became flesh and dwelt among us, and we beheld His glory, the glory as of the only begotten of the Father, full of grace and truth.

¹⁵ John bore witness of Him and cried out, saying, "This was He of whom I said, 'He who comes after me is preferred before me, for He was before me.' "

¹⁶ And of His fullness we have all received, and grace for grace. ¹⁷ For the law was given through Moses, but grace and truth came through Jesus Christ. ¹⁸ No one has seen God at any time. The only begotten Son, who is in the bosom of the Father, He has declared Him.

---

1. Read Genesis 1:1 and John 1:1. What similarities do you note between the verses? What do you think is the first point John wanted his readers to understand?

....

....

....

....

....

....

2. Although the entire nation of Israel did not accept Jesus as the Messiah, there were some who did receive Him. What does John say these people received (see verses 12–13)?

_____

_____

_____

The First Disciples (John 1:35–51)

³⁵ Again, the next day, John stood with two of his disciples. ³⁶ And looking at Jesus as He walked, he said, "Behold the Lamb of God!"

³⁷ The two disciples heard him speak, and they followed Jesus. ³⁸ Then Jesus turned, and seeing them following, said to them, "What do you seek?"

They said to Him, "Rabbi" (which is to say, when translated, Teacher), "where are You staying?"

³⁹ He said to them, "Come and see." They came and saw where He was staying, and remained with Him that day (now it was about the tenth hour).

⁴⁰ One of the two who heard John speak, and followed Him, was Andrew, Simon Peter's brother. ⁴¹ He first found his own brother Simon, and said to him, "We have found the Messiah" (which is translated, the Christ). ⁴² And he brought him to Jesus.

Now when Jesus looked at him, He said, "You are Simon the son of Jonah. You shall be called Cephas" (which is translated, A Stone).

⁴³ The following day Jesus wanted to go to Galilee, and He found Philip and said to him, "Follow Me." ⁴⁴ Now Philip was from Bethsaida, the city of Andrew and Peter. ⁴⁵ Philip found Nathanael and said to him, "We have found Him of whom Moses in the law, and also the prophets, wrote—Jesus of Nazareth, the son of Joseph."

⁴⁶ And Nathanael said to him, "Can anything good come out of Nazareth?"

Philip said to him, "Come and see."

[47] Jesus saw Nathanael coming toward Him, and said of him, "Behold, an Israelite indeed, in whom is no deceit!"

[48] Nathanael said to Him, "How do You know me?"

Jesus answered and said to him, "Before Philip called you, when you were under the fig tree, I saw you."

[49] Nathanael answered and said to Him, "Rabbi, You are the Son of God! You are the King of Israel!"

[50] Jesus answered and said to him, "Because I said to you, 'I saw you under the fig tree,' do you believe? You will see greater things than these." [51] And He said to him, "Most assuredly, I say to you, hereafter you shall see heaven open, and the angels of God ascending and descending upon the Son of Man."

---

3. What compelled Andrew to begin following Christ? How did he convince his brother, Simon (known as Peter), to also become one of Jesus' disciples (see verses 35–42)?

_____

_____

_____

_____

4. Nathanael was skeptical that the promised Messiah could come from Nazareth. After all, the town was never mentioned once in the Old Testament, and it was best known for housing Roman soldiers. How did Philip respond to Nathanael's skepticism? How did Jesus show Nathanael that something good *could* come from Nazareth (see verses 46–49)?

_____

_____

_____

_____

Jesus Changes Water into Wine (John 2:1–10)

¹ On the third day there was a wedding in Cana of Galilee, and the mother of Jesus was there. ² Now both Jesus and His disciples were invited to the wedding. ³ And when they ran out of wine, the mother of Jesus said to Him, "They have no wine."

⁴ Jesus said to her, "Woman, what does your concern have to do with Me? My hour has not yet come."

⁵ His mother said to the servants, "Whatever He says to you, do it."

⁶ Now there were set there six waterpots of stone, according to the manner of purification of the Jews, containing twenty or thirty gallons apiece. ⁷ Jesus said to them, "Fill the waterpots with water." And they filled them up to the brim. ⁸ And He said to them, "Draw some out now, and take it to the master of the feast." And they took it. ⁹ When the master of the feast had tasted the water that was made wine, and did not know where it came from (but the servants who had drawn the water knew), the master of the feast called the bridegroom. ¹⁰ And he said to him, "Every man at the beginning sets out the good wine, and when the guests have well drunk, then the inferior. You have kept the good wine until now!"

5. As far as we know, Jesus had not yet performed a public miracle . . . and His reply to His mother seems to suggest that He wasn't ready to start. Why then do you think Mary told the servants to do whatever Jesus said to them (see verses 3–5)?

6. Hospitality was extremely important in ancient Israel. To run out of wine in the middle of a wedding feast would have been humiliating for the host. How did Jesus' miracle help the bridegroom to not be embarrassed in front of his guests (see verses 6–10)?

_____

_____

_____

_____

_____

Jesus Clears the Temple Courts (John 2:13–25)

13 Now the Passover of the Jews was at hand, and Jesus went up to Jerusalem. 14 And He found in the temple those who sold oxen and sheep and doves, and the money changers doing business. 15 When He had made a whip of cords, He drove them all out of the temple, with the sheep and the oxen, and poured out the changers' money and overturned the tables. 16 And He said to those who sold doves, "Take these things away! Do not make My Father's house a house of merchandise!" 17 Then His disciples remembered that it was written, "Zeal for Your house has eaten Me up."

18 So the Jews answered and said to Him, "What sign do You show to us, since You do these things?"

19 Jesus answered and said to them, "Destroy this temple, and in three days I will raise it up."

20 Then the Jews said, "It has taken forty-six years to build this temple, and will You raise it up in three days?"

21 But He was speaking of the temple of His body. 22 Therefore, when He had risen from the dead, His disciples remembered that He had said this to them; and they believed the Scripture and the word which Jesus had said.

²³ Now when He was in Jerusalem at the Passover, during the feast, many believed in His name when they saw the signs which He did. ²⁴ But Jesus did not commit Himself to them, because He knew all men, ²⁵ and had no need that anyone should testify of man, for He knew what was in man.

---

7. Read Psalm 69:8–9. How did Jesus show "zeal" for His Father's house (see John 2:13–17)?

_____

_____

_____

_____

_____

_____

_____

8. How did Jesus respond when the religious leaders asked for a "sign" to prove His authority? What significance did Jesus' words have later for the disciples (see verses 18–22)?

_____

_____

_____

_____

_____

_____

_____

_____

REVIEWING THE STORY

The apostle John begins his Gospel by revealing the truth about Jesus' divine nature and then introduces John the Baptist, the prophesied fore-runner who would bear witness to the coming of the Messiah. John the Baptist pointed two of his own disciples, Andrew and John, to Jesus. These men, in turn, introduced their brothers, Simon (Peter) and James, to Jesus. Philip recruited Nathanael, and the band of disciples began to grow. Jesus revealed Himself as the Messiah in a relatively private way by turning water to wine at a wedding feast in Cana, and then in a very public way by driving merchants from the temple.

9. How does John describe the coming of Jesus into the world (see John 1:14)?

_____

_____

_____

_____

_____

_____

_____

10. What "greater things" did Jesus tell Nathanael that he would see (see John 1:50–51)?

_____

_____

_____

_____

_____

_____

11. How did Jesus reply when His mother, Mary, told Him the wine had run out at the wedding they were attending in Cana (see John 2:3–4)? What did He mean by this statement?

_____

_____

_____

_____

_____

12. How did Jesus react to the people who believed in Him only because of the miracles He performed (see John 2:24–25)?

_____

_____

_____

_____

_____

APPLYING THE MESSAGE

13. Nathanael almost rejected Jesus because He was from the town of Nazareth. What are some reasons why people reject Jesus today?

_____

_____

_____

_____

_____

14. Jesus was bold and zealous for the sanctity of God's house. How do you show zeal and boldness for the things of God?

_____

_____

_____

_____

_____

_____

REFLECTING ON THE MEANING

Philip brought extraordinary news to his friend Nathanael: "We have found Him of whom Moses in the law, and also the prophets, wrote— Jesus of Nazareth, the son of Joseph." Nathanael, for his part, was less than impressed. "Can anything good come out of Nazareth?" he replied (John 1:45–46).

Philip could have responded to Nathanael's skepticism and reluctance in any number of ways. He could have argued with him. He could have reasoned with him. He could have countered Nathanael's sarcasm with sarcasm of his own. Instead, he offered a simple, yet profound, three-word invitation: "Come and see" (verse 46).

What is it we do as Christians when we witness to people . . . whether it's through personal testimony, preaching, or some other action? We simply point them to Jesus. We say to them, "Come and see. Come to church with me, and you will see. Come to my Bible study, and you will see. Come to our prayer meeting, and you will see. Just come and see."

Sometimes, when we study God's Word and the theological principles it contains, we're tempted to take a more intellectual approach to our faith. We fool ourselves into thinking that if we can just find the right answers to all the questions that unbelievers have about faith in Jesus, we can somehow convince them to become Christians. Unfortunately, that is not the case at all. You cannot reason somebody to heaven.

So don't let anybody tell you that if you haven't studied apologetics or mastered theological debate, you cannot win people to Jesus. All you need is a heart for others and a confidence in the Holy Spirit. All you have to be able to say is, "Come and see." That's it! Come and see. Jesus is the self-authenticating Christ. He will take care of the rest. All you need to do is introduce Him: "Behold! The Lamb of God who takes away the sin of the world" (verse 29).

Journaling Your Response

What is keeping you from saying "come and see" to someone you know?

WHOEVER BELIEVES IN HIM

John 3:1–4:54

GETTING STARTED

What are some of the ways that you see people searching for truth today?

SETTING THE STAGE

Jesus' life was punctuated by public and personal encounters with people from all different backgrounds and walks of life. As you read the narratives in the Gospels of His three years of ministry, you can't help but notice that He spent much of His time talking with people about how to find salvation. Wherever Jesus went, He had one thing on His mind: to seek lost men and women and bring them to a saving knowledge of God through faith.

Jesus had great insights into humanity's condition. In one story, John relates in his Gospel how a man named Nicodemus came seeking answers from Jesus. Nicodemus was a Pharisee, a wealthy member of the Sanhedrin—a ruler of the Jews—who lived in the highest level of religious life in his day. But he came to Jesus by night and said, "Rabbi, we know that You are a teacher come from God; for no one can do these signs that You do unless God is with Him" (John 3:2). In that very statement, we see the searching heart of this religious leader.

Yet Nicodemus was wrong in his initial statement to Jesus. His theology wasn't correct, because Jesus wasn't just a *teacher who came from God*—He was *God who came to teach*. Nicodemus would come to recognize before the end of the conversation that he wasn't simply dealing with a representative of God. He was dealing with God in a body—Jesus Christ, the Lord of glory.

EXPLORING THE TEXT

The New Birth (John 3:1–21)

> [1] There was a man of the Pharisees named Nicodemus, a ruler of the Jews. [2] This man came to Jesus by night and said to Him, "Rabbi, we know that You are a teacher come from God; for no one can do these signs that You do unless God is with him."
>
> [3] Jesus answered and said to him, "Most assuredly, I say to you, unless one is born again, he cannot see the kingdom of God."

[4] Nicodemus said to Him, "How can a man be born when he is old? Can he enter a second time into his mother's womb and be born?"

[5] Jesus answered, "Most assuredly, I say to you, unless one is born of water and the Spirit, he cannot enter the kingdom of God. [6] That which is born of the flesh is flesh, and that which is born of the Spirit is spirit. [7] Do not marvel that I said to you, 'You must be born again.' [8] The wind blows where it wishes, and you hear the sound of it, but cannot tell where it comes from and where it goes. So is everyone who is born of the Spirit."

[9] Nicodemus answered and said to Him, "How can these things be?"

[10] Jesus answered and said to him, "Are you the teacher of Israel, and do not know these things? [11] Most assuredly, I say to you, We speak what We know and testify what We have seen, and you do not receive Our witness. [12] If I have told you earthly things and you do not believe, how will you believe if I tell you heavenly things? [13] No one has ascended to heaven but He who came down from heaven, *that is*, the Son of Man who is in heaven. [14] And as Moses lifted up the serpent in the wilderness, even so must the Son of Man be lifted up, [15] that whoever believes in Him should not perish but have eternal life.

[16] "For God so loved the world that He gave His only begotten Son, that whoever believes in Him should not perish but have everlasting life. [17] For God did not send His Son into the world to condemn the world, but that the world through Him might be saved."

[18] "He who believes in Him is not condemned; but he who does not believe is condemned already, because he has not believed in the name of the only begotten Son of God. [19] And this is the condemnation, that the light has come into the world, and men loved darkness rather than light, because their deeds were evil. [20] For everyone practicing evil hates the light and does not come to the light, lest his deeds should be exposed. [21] But he who does the truth

comes to the light, that his deeds may be clearly seen, that they have been done in God."

___

1. Look at Matthew 22:15–16. What made Nicodemus different from the other Pharisees of his day (see John 3:1–2)?

2. What did Jesus say a person had to experience to enter the kingdom of God? How did Jesus say a person could obtain eternal life (see verses 3–8, 15–16)?

John Testifies About Jesus (John 3:25–36)

25 Then there arose a dispute between some of John's disciples and the Jews about purification. 26 And they came to John and said to him, "Rabbi, He who was with you beyond the Jordan, to whom you have testified—behold, He is baptizing, and all are coming to Him!"

27 John answered and said, "A man can receive nothing unless it has been given to him from heaven. 28 You yourselves bear me witness, that I said, 'I am not the Christ,' but, 'I have been sent before Him.' 29 He who has the bride is the bridegroom; but the friend of the

bridegroom, who stands and hears him, rejoices greatly because of the bridegroom's voice. Therefore this joy of mine is fulfilled. [30] He must increase, but I must decrease. [31] He who comes from above is above all; he who is of the earth is earthly and speaks of the earth. He who comes from heaven is above all. [32] And what He has seen and heard, that He testifies; and no one receives His testimony. [33] He who has received His testimony has certified that God is true. [34] For He whom God has sent speaks the words of God, for God does not give the Spirit by measure. [35] The Father loves the Son, and has given all things into His hand. [36] He who believes in the Son has everlasting life; and he who does not believe the Son shall not see life, but the wrath of God abides on him."

---

3. It is likely that John's disciples were concerned about the growing popularity of Jesus' ministry—and that people were going to Christ for baptism rather than to John. How did John respond to these concerns (see verses 27–30)?

_____

_____

_____

_____

_____

4. What message did John have for those who refused to believe in Jesus (see verse 36)?

_____

_____

_____

_____

_____

Jesus Speaks with a Samaritan Woman (John 4:5–26)

[5] So He came to a city of Samaria which is called Sychar, near the plot of ground that Jacob gave to his son Joseph. [6] Now Jacob's well was there. Jesus therefore, being wearied from His journey, sat thus by the well. It was about the sixth hour.

[7] A woman of Samaria came to draw water. Jesus said to her, "Give Me a drink." [8] For His disciples had gone away into the city to buy food.

[9] Then the woman of Samaria said to Him, "How is it that You, being a Jew, ask a drink from me, a Samaritan woman?" For Jews have no dealings with Samaritans.

[10] Jesus answered and said to her, "If you knew the gift of God, and who it is who says to you, 'Give Me a drink,' you would have asked Him, and He would have given you living water."

[11] The woman said to Him, "Sir, You have nothing to draw with, and the well is deep. Where then do You get that living water? [12] Are You greater than our father Jacob, who gave us the well, and drank from it himself, as well as his sons and his livestock?"

[13] Jesus answered and said to her, "Whoever drinks of this water will thirst again, [14] but whoever drinks of the water that I shall give him will never thirst. But the water that I shall give him will become in him a fountain of water springing up into everlasting life."

[15] The woman said to Him, "Sir, give me this water, that I may not thirst, nor come here to draw."

[16] Jesus said to her, "Go, call your husband, and come here."

[17] The woman answered and said, "I have no husband."

Jesus said to her, "You have well said, 'I have no husband,' [18] for you have had five husbands, and the one whom you now have is not your husband; in that you spoke truly."

[19] The woman said to Him, "Sir, I perceive that You are a prophet. [20] Our fathers worshiped on this mountain, and you Jews say that in Jerusalem is the place where one ought to worship."

21 Jesus said to her, "Woman, believe Me, the hour is coming when you will neither on this mountain, nor in Jerusalem, worship the Father. 22 You worship what you do not know; we know what we worship, for salvation is of the Jews. 23 But the hour is coming, and now is, when the true worshipers will worship the Father inspirit and truth; for the Father is seeking such to worship Him. 24 God is Spirit, and those who worship Him must worship in spirit and truth."

25 The woman said to Him, "I know that Messiah is coming" (who is called Christ). "When He comes, He will tell us all things."

26 Jesus said to her, "I who speak to you am He."

---

5. Why did Jesus' request for water surprise the Samaritan woman? How did Jesus respond to her question (see verses 9–10)?

_____

_____

_____

_____

_____

_____

_____

6. What did Jesus reveal about this woman's past that made her believe He was a prophet (see verses 16–20)?

_____

_____

_____

_____

_____

_____

_____

A Nobleman's Son Healed (John 4:39–53)

[39] And many of the Samaritans of that city believed in Him because of the word of the woman who testified, "He told me all that I ever did." [40] So when the Samaritans had come to Him, they urged Him to stay with them; and He stayed there two days. [41] And many more believed because of His own word.

[42] Then they said to the woman, "Now we believe, not because of what you said, for we ourselves have heard Him and we know that this is indeed the Christ, the Savior of the world."

[43] Now after the two days He departed from there and went to Galilee. [44] For Jesus Himself testified that a prophet has no honor in his own country. [45] So when He came to Galilee, the Galileans received Him, having seen all the things He did in Jerusalem at the feast; for they also had gone to the feast.

[46] So Jesus came again to Cana of Galilee where He had made the water wine. And there was a certain nobleman whose son was sick at Capernaum. [47] When he heard that Jesus had come out of Judea into Galilee, he went to Him and implored Him to come down and heal his son, for he was at the point of death. [48] Then Jesus said to him, "Unless you people see signs and wonders, you will by no means believe."

[49] The nobleman said to Him, "Sir, come down before my child dies!"

[50] Jesus said to him, "Go your way; your son lives." So the man believed the word that Jesus spoke to him, and he went his way. [51] And as he was now going down, his servants met him and told him, saying, "Your son lives!"

[52] Then he inquired of them the hour when he got better. And they said to him, "Yesterday at the seventh hour the fever left him." [53] So the father knew that it was at the same hour in which Jesus said to him, "Your son lives." And he himself believed, and his whole household.

7. Read Luke 7:2–10. What was the difference between the faith the centurion demonstrated and the faith of the nobleman in this passage?

_____

_____

_____

_____

_____

_____

8. How did the nobleman confirm that it was Jesus who healed his son (see verses 52–53)?

_____

_____

_____

_____

_____

REVIEWING THE STORY

As Jesus' earthly ministry grew, people began to recognize that He was different from the other teachers of the day. Nicodemus, a Pharisee, recognized God's unmistakable power through Christ and wanted to know more about His message. John the Baptist recognized Jesus as the One who had come from above and was only too overjoyed to cede the limelight to Him. A Samaritan woman recognized Jesus as a prophet—and much more—after only a brief conversation with Him. A nobleman from Capernaum recognized Jesus as a healer who could save his son. All of them were right . . . but none of them could fully grasp Jesus' true identity.

9. Why do you think Jesus' reply to Nicodemus in John 3:16 is perhaps the best-known verse in the Bible? How does this verse summarize Jesus' mission to our world?

_____

_____

_____

_____

10. What did John the Baptist say was the core purpose of his ministry (see John 3:28–36)?

_____

_____

_____

_____

11. How did Jesus respond when the Samaritan woman said that she perceived He was a prophet (see John 4:21–26)?

_____

_____

_____

_____

12. When Jesus healed the son of the nobleman from Capernaum, He did not accompany the man back to his home but simply said, "your son lives." What act of faith would this have required on the nobleman's part to accept Jesus at His word (see John 4:49–51)?

_____

_____

_____

APPLYING THE MESSAGE

13. John the Baptist said, "Jesus must increase and I must decrease" (John 3:30). What would it look like for you to apply this principle to your life today?

_____

_____

_____

_____

14. Many people came to believe in Jesus because the Samaritan woman testified, "He told me all that I ever did" (John 4:39). If you told others about your personal experience with Christ, what are some the things you would share that He had done for you?

_____

_____

_____

_____

REFLECTING ON THE MEANING

There are at least three takeaways from Jesus' healing of the nobleman's son in John 4:46–54. The first is that when we believe God, *our faith allows Him to operate in any way He chooses.* As Christians, we tend to think we can "control" God. We say to Him (in so many words), "This is what You need to do for me, and this is exactly how You need to do it." We give Him step-by-step instructions to follow, and then we're left confused when He does something His own way. But the Lord isn't bound to our methods or our schedule. If we have faith, we will not make Him subject to our understanding of how to deal with a situation.

The second takeaway is that *faith acts first and then sees the results.* The nobleman did not have the option of waiting to see evidence before he believed. He had to take the steps of faith that were inscribed on his heart in the moment. When he did, he saw the results. If all we have in our spiritual lives is what we have witnessed before we believed, then we really don't have anything. Faith acts first . . . and then sees the results.

The third takeaway is that in times of difficulty, sorrow, and unexplained tragedy, *faith accepts that God is at work even before we can see what He is doing*. Isn't that the hardest thing that God asks us to do? We come to Him with an urgent prayer and say, "Lord, You know our need. We ask You to deal with it according to Your will." But if we don't see results immediately, we're tempted to assume God isn't doing *anything*. Only later do we discover that while we were praying, He had already set His response into motion.

JOURNALING YOUR RESPONSE

What is the best story from your life that confirms "God works in mysterious ways"?

THE BREAD OF LIFE
John 5:1–6:71

GETTING STARTED

How long can you go without physical nourishment (food) before you start to feel the effects? How long can you go without spiritual nourishment before you start to feel the effects?

SETTING THE STAGE

The third miracle of Jesus that John records in his Gospel is the healing of the man at the pool of Bethesda (see John 5:1–9). This miracle is pivotal to John's narrative because it initiates a change in how the Jewish people began to react to Him. Up to this point Jesus had been well received, but now He will begin to be confronted by the people's unbelief and hostility. This sentiment will only intensify as His ministry progresses.

What Jesus does in this chapter of John's Gospel is what eventually leads to His death. It begins when Jesus takes pity on an invalid—a man who had no way to help himself and had no one else to help him. The problem was that Jesus helped the man on the *Sabbath* . . . and the Jewish leaders could not excuse Him for violating their restrictions against working on that day. In their zeal to protect their Sabbath rules, they ignored the undeniable miracle that had taken place right before their eyes. Jesus demonstrated His power over sickness and His ability to heal a person who had been unable to walk for thirty-eight years.

The miracle took place in Jerusalem during "a feast of the Jews" (verse 1), but John doesn't specify whether this was the feast for Passover (March–April), Pentecost (fifty-two days later), or Tabernacles (September–October). Regardless, this would have been a time of happiness and celebration for the Jewish people . . . or at least for most of them. Jesus, however, went to a place in the city where few were celebrating.

The Pool of Bethesda was fed by an underground spring, which occasionally stirred the waters (though some thought an angel was responsible). People believed the water in the pool had a healing effect, so all manner of blind, disabled, and sick people gathered there. This is where Jesus went, and this is where the reactions to Him changed quickly and dramatically.

Exploring the Text

A Man Healed at the Pool of Bethesda (John 5:1–15)

¹ After this there was a feast of the Jews, and Jesus went up to Jerusalem. ² Now there is in Jerusalem by the Sheep Gate a pool, which is called in Hebrew, Bethesda, having five porches. ³ In these lay a great multitude of sick people, blind, lame, paralyzed, waiting for the moving of the water. ⁴ For an angel went down at a certain

time into the pool and stirred up the water; then whoever stepped in first, after the stirring of the water, was made well of whatever disease he had. [5] Now a certain man was there who had an infirmity thirty-eight years. [6] When Jesus saw him lying there, and knew that he already had been in that condition a long time, He said to him, "Do you want to be made well?"

[7] The sick man answered Him, "Sir, I have no man to put me into the pool when the water is stirred up; but while I am coming, another steps down before me."

[8] Jesus said to him, "Rise, take up your bed and walk." [9] And immediately the man was made well, took up his bed, and walked.

And that day was the Sabbath. [10] The Jews therefore said to him who was cured, "It is the Sabbath; it is not lawful for you to carry your bed."

[11] He answered them, "He who made me well said to me, 'Take up your bed and walk.' "

[12] Then they asked him, "Who is the Man who said to you, 'Take up your bed and walk'?" [13] But the one who was healed did not know who it was, for Jesus had withdrawn, a multitude being in that place. [14] Afterward Jesus found him in the temple, and said to him, "See, you have been made well. Sin no more, lest a worse thing come upon you."

[15] The man departed and told the Jews that it was Jesus who had made him well.

---

1. Why did the multitude of sick, blind, lame, and paralyzed people mentioned in this passage lay beside the Pool of Bethesda (see verses 3–4)?

2. The Pharisees did not care that a man who had been immobile for thirty-eight years was suddenly able to walk. What was their greatest concern about the man (see verses 9–10)?

_____

_____

_____

_____

The Authority of the Son (John 5:16–30)

¹⁶ For this reason the Jews persecuted Jesus, and sought to kill Him, because He had done these things on the Sabbath. ¹⁷ But Jesus answered them, "My Father has been working until now, and I have been working."

¹⁸ Therefore the Jews sought all the more to kill Him, because He not only broke the Sabbath, but also said that God was His Father, making Himself equal with God. ¹⁹ Then Jesus answered and said to them, "Most assuredly, I say to you, the Son can do nothing of Himself, but what He sees the Father do; for whatever He does, the Son also does in like manner. ²⁰ For the Father loves the Son, and shows Him all things that He Himself does; and He will show Him greater works than these, that you may marvel. ²¹ For as the Father raises the dead and gives life to them, even so the Son gives life to whom He will. ²² For the Father judges no one, but has committed all judgment to the Son, ²³ that all should honor the Son just as they honor the Father. He who does not honor the Son does not honor the Father who sent Him.

²⁴ "Most assuredly, I say to you, he who hears My word and believes in Him who sent Me has everlasting life, and shall not come into judgment, but has passed from death into life. ²⁵ Most assuredly, I say to you, the hour is coming, and now is, when the dead will hear the voice of the Son of God; and those who hear will live. ²⁶ For as

the Father has life in Himself, so He has granted the Son to have life in Himself, [27] and has given Him authority to execute judgment also, because He is the Son of Man. [28] Do not marvel at this; for the hour is coming in which all who are in the graves will hear His voice [29] and come forth—those who have done good, to the resurrection of life, and those who have done evil, to the resurrection of condemnation. [30] I can of Myself do nothing. As I hear, I judge; and My judgment is righteous, because I do not seek My own will but the will of the Father who sent Me.

3. What caused the Jewish leaders to suddenly desire to kill Jesus (see verses 16–18)?

_____

_____

_____

_____

_____

4. What authority did Jesus claim that God the Father had given to Him (see verses 24–27)?

_____

_____

_____

_____

Jesus Feeds the Five Thousand (John 6:1–15)

[1] After these things Jesus went over the Sea of Galilee, which is the Sea of Tiberias. [2] Then a great multitude followed Him, because they saw His signs which He performed on those who were diseased. [3] And Jesus went up on the mountain, and there He sat with His disciples.

⁴ Now the Passover, a feast of the Jews, was near. ⁵ Then Jesus lifted up His eyes, and seeing a great multitude coming toward Him, He said to Philip, "Where shall we buy bread, that these may eat?" ⁶ But this He said to test him, for He Himself knew what He would do.

⁷ Philip answered Him, "Two hundred denarii worth of bread is not sufficient for them, that every one of them may have a little."

⁸ One of His disciples, Andrew, Simon Peter's brother, said to Him, ⁹ "There is a lad here who has five barley loaves and two small fish, but what are they among so many?"

¹⁰ Then Jesus said, "Make the people sit down." Now there was much grass in the place. So the men sat down, in number about five thousand. ¹¹ And Jesus took the loaves, and when He had given thanks He distributed them to the disciples, and the disciples to those sitting down; and likewise of the fish, as much as they wanted. ¹² So when they were filled, He said to His disciples, "Gather up the fragments that remain, so that nothing is lost." ¹³ Therefore they gathered them up, and filled twelve baskets with the fragments of the five barley loaves which were left over by those who had eaten. ¹⁴ Then those men, when they had seen the sign that Jesus did, said, "This is truly the Prophet who is to come into the world."

¹⁵ Therefore when Jesus perceived that they were about to come and take Him by force to make Him king, He departed again to the mountain by Himself alone.

---

5. What question did Jesus ask Philip in order to "test" him? What solution to the problem did Andrew provide (see verses 5–9)?

_____

_____

_____

_____

_____

6. How did the people react when they witnessed this miracle of Jesus? How did this cause Jesus to retreat to the mountain alone (see verses 14–15)?

The Bread of Life (John 6:41–60)

⁴¹ The Jews then complained about Him, because He said, "I am the bread which came down from heaven." ⁴² And they said, "Is not this Jesus, the son of Joseph, whose father and mother we know? How is it then that He says, 'I have come down from heaven'?"

⁴³ Jesus therefore answered and said to them, "Do not murmur among yourselves. ⁴⁴ No one can come to Me unless the Father who sent Me draws him; and I will raise him up at the last day. ⁴⁵ It is written in the prophets, 'And they shall all be taught by God.' Therefore everyone who has heard and learned from the Father comes to Me. ⁴⁶ Not that anyone has seen the Father, except He who is from God; He has seen the Father. ⁴⁷ Most assuredly, I say to you, he who believes in Me has everlasting life. ⁴⁸ I am the bread of life. ⁴⁹ Your fathers ate the manna in the wilderness, and are dead. ⁵⁰ This is the bread which comes down from heaven, that one may eat of it and not die. ⁵¹ I am the living bread which came down from heaven. If anyone eats of this bread, he will live forever; and the bread that I shall give is My flesh, which I shall give for the life of the world."

⁵² The Jews therefore quarreled among themselves, saying, "How can this Man give us His flesh to eat?"

⁵³ Then Jesus said to them, "Most assuredly, I say to you, unless you eat the flesh of the Son of Man and drink His blood, you have no life in you. ⁵⁴ Whoever eats My flesh and drinks My blood has

eternal life, and I will raise him up at the last day. [55] For My flesh is food indeed, and My blood is drink indeed. [56] He who eats My flesh and drinks My blood abides in Me, and I in him. [57] As the living Father sent Me, and I live because of the Father, so he who feeds on Me will live because of Me. [58] This is the bread which came down from heaven—not as your fathers ate the manna, and are dead. He who eats this bread will live forever."

[59] These things He said in the synagogue as He taught in Capernaum.

[60] Therefore many of His disciples, when they heard this, said, "This is a hard saying; who can understand it?"

---

7. What did Jesus mean when He said that He was the bread of life (see verses 48–51?)

_____

_____

_____

_____

_____

_____

8. Why was this teaching difficult for many of the people to grasp? What did they do as a result (see verses 52, 60)?

_____

_____

_____

_____

_____

_____

REVIEWING THE STORY

Nicodemus, the religious leader who came to see Jesus at night, referred to Him as "a teacher come from God" (John 3:2). His middle-ground statement revealed that He acknowledged Jesus' supernatural power but ignored His claims to be the Messiah. As the stories in John 5–6 reveal, Jesus quickly removed any such "wiggle room." He spoke of His identity as God the Son who would one day judge the righteous and the unrighteous. He demonstrated His divine power by performing many more miracles. His words and deeds strengthened the faith of some followers, but alienated many others . . . and also served to enrage His enemies.

9. Why do you think Jesus asked the man beside the Pool of Bethesda whether he wanted to be made well before healing him (see John 5:6)?

10. The Jewish leaders began plotting to kill Jesus when He healed this man on the Sabbath. What did Jesus say to them that served to intensify their desire to kill Him (see John 5:17)?

11. How did the disciples demonstrate their lack of faith when Jesus tested them by asking where they would buy food to feed the five thousand (see John 6:5–9)?

_____

_____

_____

_____

12. How was Jesus, the bread of life who came from heaven, different from manna, the bread from heaven that the Israelites ate in the wilderness (see John 6:49, 58)?

_____

_____

_____

_____

APPLYING THE MESSAGE

13. The man who lay beside the Pool of Bethesda had been seeking healing for some time, and his response to Jesus indicates he had all but given up hope. In what ways can you relate to his feeling? What are some areas of your life where you are waiting for healing?

_____

_____

_____

_____

_____

14. Many of Jesus' followers struggled with the idea that He is the bread of life. Which of His teachings are especially hard for you to understand, accept, or follow? Why?

REFLECTING ON THE MEANING

Jesus' feeding of the 5,000 is one of seven miracles around which John structures his Gospel. In a remote area, Jesus used the meager provisions of a young boy to feed thousands of hungry people. John's account illustrates Jesus' loving concern for the multitude as well as His authority and power. It also raises a few important questions for us as His followers.

The first question the episode asks us to consider is *what resources we have that God can use.* Every follower of Christ has a gift. Some of us have the gift of song. Some of us have the gift of compassion. Some of us have the gift of mercy. Some of us have the gift of ministry. Others of us may feel we don't have much to offer . . . but that's not the point. The point is that we are willing to offer God what we *do* have, just as the boy did with the loaves and fish.

The second question the story asks us to consider is *whether we have asked God to bless the resources we have to give.* John writes that Jesus took the little boy's lunch and prayed over it, and that is when the miracle occurred—when Jesus asked God to bless the food. We can have all the giftedness in the world. We can be the most talented of people in our community. But God is not going to use our talents until we take them to Him and ask Him to bless them.

The third question the account compels us to ask is *whether we are willing to allow God to use our resources for His glory.* The final step is to put what we have into circulation. When we choose to do this, we are saying, in effect, "Lord God, here is my gift. Please bless it. It is yours. Do with it as you please."

Make these questions personal today. What do *you* have to offer God? Have you given it to Jesus? Have you asked Him to bless it? Are you willing for Him to take your gift and use it any way He wants? If so, prepare for your gift to be multiplied and used to bless others.

JOURNALING YOUR RESPONSE

Which of your spiritual gifts do you need to turn over to God for His blessing and use? What do you think God could do with those spiritual gifts?

HOSTILE REACTIONS

John 7:1–8:59

GETTING STARTED

What is your relationship like with your family members? What are some ways your family members handle conflicts with one another?

_____

_____

_____

_____

_____

_____

_____

_____

_____

_____

_____

_____

SETTING THE STAGE

Jesus had been ministering in Galilee, where He had received a mostly favorable response. But as the nature of His teaching became understood, the crowds began to dwindle. Eventually, He was left with only His disciples,

His brothers, and a handful of other followers. Jesus seemed unwilling to leave Galilee. He stayed there for some time, perhaps as long as six months.

Jesus did not want to venture into Judea, with its large Jewish population, because He knew that many of the Jewish religious leaders there wanted to kill Him. It's not that Jesus was afraid of these religious leaders, or that He was afraid of death. He had just recognized that the time for His impending death had not yet arrived. But at some point, His brothers confronted Him about His self-imposed exile. These men were actually His *half*-brothers, the sons of Mary by Joseph. At this point in the biblical narrative, they didn't believe Jesus was the Messiah.

The brothers suggested a dangerous course of action. In essence, they told Jesus, "You have been here in Galilee, and the crowds are leaving. You had better get back to Jerusalem and do some good things in front of a large crowd. If You don't, Your whole ministry will be over. See if You can get some people to follow You again. You're here by Yourself, and no great leader ever accomplishes anything all by himself."

Jesus' reply was pointed and emphatic. He said, in essence, "I will not go, because it is not time yet." Jesus lived His life in absolute conformity to the schedule of His Father. He was on a carefully orchestrated mission. Every move was planned from heaven . . . and Jesus followed that plan to the letter.

EXPLORING THE TEXT

Jesus' Brothers Disbelieve (John 7:1–19)

---

¹ After these things Jesus walked in Galilee; for He did not want to walk in Judea, because the Jews sought to kill Him. ² Now the Jews' Feast of Tabernacles was at hand. ³ His brothers therefore said to Him, "Depart from here and go into Judea, that Your disciples also may see the works that You are doing. ⁴ For no one does anything in secret while he himself seeks to be known openly. If You do these things, show Yourself to the world." ⁵ For even His brothers did not believe in Him.

⁶ Then Jesus said to them, "My time has not yet come, but your time is always ready. ⁷ The world cannot hate you, but it hates Me because I testify of it that its works are evil. ⁸ You go up to this feast. I am not yet going up to this feast, for My time has not yet fully come." ⁹ When He had said these things to them, He remained in Galilee.

¹⁰ But when His brothers had gone up, then He also went up to the feast, not openly, but as it were in secret. ¹¹ Then the Jews sought Him at the feast, and said, "Where is He?" ¹² And there was much complaining among the people concerning Him. Some said, "He is good"; others said, "No, on the contrary, He deceives the people." ¹³ However, no one spoke openly of Him for fear of the Jews.

¹⁴ Now about the middle of the feast Jesus went up into the temple and taught. ¹⁵ And the Jews marveled, saying, "How does this Man know letters, having never studied?"

¹⁶ Jesus answered them and said, "My doctrine is not Mine, but His who sent Me. ¹⁷ If anyone wills to do His will, he shall know concerning the doctrine, whether it is from God or whether I speak on My own authority. ¹⁸ He who speaks from himself seeks his own glory; but He who seeks the glory of the One who sent Him is true, and no unrighteousness is in Him. ¹⁹ Did not Moses give you the law, yet none of you keeps the law? Why do you seek to kill Me?"

1. Jesus had remained in His home region of Galilee because the Jewish leaders in Judea wanted to kill Him. What advice did His brothers give to Him at this point (see verses 3–5)?

---

2. Typically, those from the towns who were going to the feasts in Jerusalem would travel there together in large caravans. Why did Jesus choose to go to the feast "in secret" and when it was already well underway (see verses 10–13)?

_____

_____

_____

_____

_____

_____

_____

Division Over Christ (John 7:32–52)

[32] The Pharisees heard the crowd murmuring these things concerning Him, and the Pharisees and the chief priests sent officers to take Him. [33] Then Jesus said to them, "I shall be with you a little while longer, and then I go to Him who sent Me. [34] You will seek Me and not find Me, and where I am you cannot come."

[35] Then the Jews said among themselves, "Where does He intend to go that we shall not find Him? Does He intend to go to the Dispersion among the Greeks and teach the Greeks? [36] What is this thing that He said, 'You will seek Me and not find Me, and where I am you cannot come'?"

[37] On the last day, that great day of the feast, Jesus stood and cried out, saying, "If anyone thirsts, let him come to Me and drink. [38] He who believes in Me, as the Scripture has said, out of his heart will flow rivers of living water." [39] But this He spoke concerning the Spirit, whom those believing in Him would receive; for the Holy Spirit was not yet given, because Jesus was not yet glorified.

[40] Therefore many from the crowd, when they heard this saying, said, "Truly this is the Prophet." [41] Others said, "This is the Christ."

But some said, "Will the Christ come out of Galilee? ⁴² Has not the Scripture said that the Christ comes from the seed of David and from the town of Bethlehem, where David was?" ⁴³ So there was a division among the people because of Him. ⁴⁴ Now some of them wanted to take Him, but no one laid hands on Him.

⁴⁵ Then the officers came to the chief priests and Pharisees, who said to them, "Why have you not brought Him?"

⁴⁶ The officers answered, "No man ever spoke like this Man!"

⁴⁷ Then the Pharisees answered them, "Are you also deceived? ⁴⁸ Have any of the rulers or the Pharisees believed in Him? ⁴⁹ But this crowd that does not know the law is accursed."

⁵⁰ Nicodemus (he who came to Jesus by night, being one of them) said to them, ⁵¹ "Does our law judge a man before it hears him and knows what he is doing?"

⁵² They answered and said to him, "Are you also from Galilee? Search and look, for no prophet has arisen out of Galilee."

---

3. Jesus was referring to His imminent death when He told the people He would be with them just a little while longer. How did the people misinterpret His words? What did they think Jesus was planning to do (see verses 33–36)?

_____

_____

_____

_____

_____

_____

_____

_____

_____

4. How did confusion over Jesus' birthplace keep some people from believing that He was the promised Messiah (see verses 41–43)?

_____

_____

_____

_____

_____

The Woman Caught in Adultery (John 8:1–12)

¹ But Jesus went to the Mount of Olives.

² Now early in the morning He came again into the temple, and all the people came to Him; and He sat down and taught them. ³ Then the scribes and Pharisees brought to Him a woman caught in adultery. And when they had set her in the midst, ⁴ they said to Him, "Teacher, this woman was caught in adultery, in the very act. ⁵ Now Moses, in the law, commanded us that such should be stoned. But what do You say?" ⁶ This they said, testing Him, that they might have something of which to accuse Him. But Jesus stooped down and wrote on the ground with His finger, as though He did not hear.

⁷ So when they continued asking Him, He raised Himself up and said to them, "He who is without sin among you, let him throw a stone at her first." ⁸ And again He stooped down and wrote on the ground. ⁹ Then those who heard it, being convicted by their conscience, went out one by one, beginning with the oldest even to the last. And Jesus was left alone, and the woman standing in the midst. ¹⁰ When Jesus had raised Himself up and saw no one but the woman, He said to her, "Woman, where are those accusers of yours? Has no one condemned you?"

¹¹ She said, "No one, Lord."

And Jesus said to her, "Neither do I condemn you; go and sin no more."

¹² Then Jesus spoke to them again, saying, "I am the light of the world. He who follows Me shall not walk in darkness, but have the light of life."

5. The scribes and Pharisees thought they had trapped Jesus. If Jesus said the woman caught in adultery should be put to death, they could have accused Him of lacking compassion for "sinners." If He said she shouldn't be killed, they could have accused Him of ignoring Old Testament law. How did Jesus evade their trap (see verses 3–8)?

_____

_____

_____

_____

6. The woman's accusers did not "condemn" her or carry out the sentence against her. How does this story illustrate God's forgiveness to all who have sinned (see verses 10–11)?

_____

_____

_____

_____

The Truth Shall Make You Free (John 8:31–59)

³¹ Then Jesus said to those Jews who believed Him, "If you abide in My word, you are My disciples indeed. ³² And you shall know the truth, and the truth shall make you free."

³³ They answered Him, "We are Abraham's descendants, and have never been in bondage to anyone. How can You say, 'You will be made free'?"

[34] Jesus answered them, "Most assuredly, I say to you, whoever commits sin is a slave of sin. [35] And a slave does not abide in the house forever, but a son abides forever. [36] Therefore if the Son makes you free, you shall be free indeed.

[37] "I know that you are Abraham's descendants, but you seek to kill Me, because My word has no place in you. [38] I speak what I have seen with My Father, and you do what you have seen with your father."

[39] They answered and said to Him, "Abraham is our father."

Jesus said to them, "If you were Abraham's children, you would do the works of Abraham. [40] But now you seek to kill Me, a Man who has told you the truth which I heard from God. Abraham did not do this. [41] You do the deeds of your father."

Then they said to Him, "We were not born of fornication; we have one Father—God."

[52] Then the Jews said to Him, "Now we know that You have a demon! Abraham is dead, and the prophets; and You say, 'If anyone keeps My word he shall never taste death.' [53] Are You greater than our father Abraham, who is dead? And the prophets are dead. Who do You make Yourself out to be?"

[54] Jesus answered, "If I honor Myself, My honor is nothing. It is My Father who honors Me, of whom you say that He is your God. [55] Yet you have not known Him, but I know Him. And if I say, 'I do not know Him,' I shall be a liar like you; but I do know Him and keep His word. [56] Your father Abraham rejoiced to see My day, and he saw it and was glad."

[57] Then the Jews said to Him, "You are not yet fifty years old, and have You seen Abraham?"

[58] Jesus said to them, "Most assuredly, I say to you, before Abraham was, I AM."

[59] Then they took up stones to throw at Him; but Jesus hid Himself and went out of the temple, going through the midst of them, and so passed by.

7. Think about the circumstances of Jesus' birth, especially Mary's conception, as recorded in Luke 1:34–38. Why do you think Jesus' enemies may have emphasized, "We were not born of fornication; we have one Father—God" (verse 41)?

_____

_____

_____

_____

_____

_____

8. Read Exodus 3:13–14. Why do you think Jesus used the words "I AM" when responding to the Jewish religious leaders? How did they react (see John 8:58–59)?

_____

_____

_____

_____

_____

_____

REVIEWING THE STORY

Jesus continued to face hostility and unbelief. The Jewish leaders were now plotting to kill Him, so He avoided their home turf of Jerusalem and remained in the region of Galilee. At one point Jesus' brothers urged Him to make Himself known to the people in Jerusalem, but ultimately they did not accept Him as the Messiah. When Jesus finally did travel to Jerusalem, His enemies pounced. They tested Him and accused Him of lying, of being a Samaritan, and of having a demon. They moved to attack Him. But ultimately, they were at the mercy of God's timetable.

9. What opinions did the Jewish people have about Jesus at the Feast of Tabernacles? Why were they afraid to voice these comments publicly (see John 7:11–13)?

_____

_____

_____

_____

10. What was Jesus' invitation to those who were spiritually thirsty? What did Jesus promise? What was the condition for receiving that promise (see John 7:37–39)?

_____

_____

_____

_____

11. Why do you think the religious leaders refused to carry out the sentence against the woman who had been caught in adultery (see John 8:7–10)?

_____

_____

_____

_____

12. The Jewish people believed they were heirs to the covenant between God and Abraham, and thus possessed the truth and were slaves to no one. How did Jesus correct their understanding? How did He say they could find true freedom (see John 8:31–36)?

_____

_____

_____

_____

APPLYING THE MESSAGE

13. What is the most Christlike way to deal with someone who—like the woman brought to Jesus—is guilty of a profound moral failure?

....

....

....

....

14. What do you think is the difference between *reading* the Bible and *abiding* in God's Word, as Jesus emphasized (see John 8:31)? What can you do to *abide* more than you *read*?

....

....

....

....

REFLECTING ON THE MEANING

When you live according to God's schedule, as Jesus did, nothing can distract you from your mission. There will always be people who will try to dissuade you from the goal you believe God wants you to accomplish. When that happens, look to Jesus for guidance.

When you live according to God's schedule, *nothing can destroy you.* Jesus' enemies tried to end His life on several occasions, but they failed each time. God already had determined the moment of Jesus' death, and no one could alter it.

When you live according to God's schedule, *nothing can discourage you.* The Pharisees called Jesus a liar. They accused Him of being a hated Samaritan. They claimed that He was possessed by a demon. Jesus confronted their accusations, spoke the truth, and refused to allow their comments to discourage Him or dissuade Him from His purpose. He could face what was to come because He was confident it was part of God's will.

When you live according to God's schedule, *nothing can disappoint you*. At one point in Jesus' ministry, many who had been following Him suddenly turned away. His own brothers expressed their disbelief in Him. And He knew His own disciples would soon abandon Him. But Jesus knew this was all part of God's greater plan. He also knew that He would never truly be alone, because His heavenly Father was always with Him.

When you live your life according to God's schedule, *nothing can defeat you*. Time and again, the scribes and the Pharisees tried to set traps for Jesus. They wanted to get Jesus to say or do something that would discredit Him in the eyes of the people . . . and make themselves look righteous. But Jesus proved to be victorious each and every time.

So look to Jesus as your example and strive to live according to God's schedule. When you do, you will find nothing can destroy you, discourage you, disappoint you, or defeat you.

JOURNALING YOUR RESPONSE

When are you most tempted to follow your own timeline instead of God's schedule?

AN EYE-OPENING EXPERIENCE

John 9:1–10:42

GETTING STARTED

What would your friends say if someone asked them what impact Jesus has had on your life?

_____

_____

_____

_____

_____

_____

_____

_____

_____

_____

_____

_____

_____

_____

_____

_____

_____

_____

Setting the Stage

The authors of the Gospels rarely reveal what happened to people after Jesus healed them. But one story, told in John 9, is as an exception. In this account, Jesus restored a blind man's sight. That singular event triggered a variety of expected and unexpected responses.

The man's neighbors reacted first. They had known the man as being blind from birth. The fact that he was now different—that his vacant stare had been replaced with a light in his expression—surprised and confused them. Some of them wondered if he was actually the same person they had known. When the man assured them he was, they had two questions: "How were your eyes opened?" and, "Where is the One who opened them?"

The Jewish religious leaders also reacted. A group of Pharisees were quickly assigned to investigate the story. The man told them how Jesus had spit on the ground, made clay, and placed the mud on his eyes. He told them how, after washing away the clay, he could see for the first time in his life. The Pharisees were livid that Jesus had done such work on the Sabbath—and they wondered how a *sinner* could do such a miracle. They tried to get the man to recant his story, but he refused. So they threw him out of the temple.

The man's parents were afraid they would also be banned from the temple. So when they were asked about their son's healing, they said only that he was their son and that he was born blind. They were afraid of what they would lose if they confirmed the miracle.

Exploring the Text

A Man Born Blind Receives Sight (John 9:1–12)

¹ Now as Jesus passed by, He saw a man who was blind from birth.
² And His disciples asked Him, saying, "Rabbi, who sinned, this man or his parents, that he was born blind?"

³ Jesus answered, "Neither this man nor his parents sinned, but that the works of God should be revealed in him. ⁴ I must work the works of Him who sent Me while it is day; the night is coming when no one can work. ⁵ As long as I am in the world, I am the light of the world."

⁶ When He had said these things, He spat on the ground and made clay with the saliva; and He anointed the eyes of the blind man with the clay. ⁷ And He said to him, "Go, wash in the pool of Siloam" (which is translated, Sent). So he went and washed, and came back seeing.

⁸ Therefore the neighbors and those who previously had seen that he was blind said, "Is not this he who sat and begged?"

⁹ Some said, "This is he." Others said, "He is like him."

He said, "I am he."

¹⁰ Therefore they said to him, "How were your eyes opened?"

¹¹ He answered and said, "A Man called Jesus made clay and anointed my eyes and said to me, 'Go to the pool of Siloam and wash.' So I went and washed, and I received sight."

¹² Then they said to him, "Where is He?"

He said, "I do not know."

---

1. What question did the disciples ask Jesus when they saw the man who was blind from birth? What assumptions did they have about the man or his parents (see verses 1–2)?

_____

_____

_____

_____

_____

_____

2. How did the man's neighbors and acquaintances respond when they realized he had been healed from his lifelong blindness (see verses 8–12)?

_____

_____

_____

_____

_____

_____

The Pharisees Investigate the Healing (John 9:16–41)

16 Therefore some of the Pharisees said, "This Man is not from God, because He does not keep the Sabbath."

Others said, "How can a man who is a sinner do such signs?" And there was a division among them.

17 They said to the blind man again, "What do you say about Him because He opened your eyes?"

He said, "He is a prophet."

18 But the Jews did not believe concerning him, that he had been blind and received his sight, until they called the parents of him who had received his sight. 19 And they asked them, saying, "Is this your son, who you say was born blind? How then does he now see?"

20 His parents answered them and said, "We know that this is our son, and that he was born blind; 21 but by what means he now sees we do not know, or who opened his eyes we do not know. He is of age; ask him. He will speak for himself." 22 His parents said these things because they feared the Jews, for the Jews had agreed already that if anyone confessed that He was Christ, he would be put out of the synagogue. 23 Therefore his parents said, "He is of age; ask him."

24 So they again called the man who was blind, and said to him, "Give God the glory! We know that this Man is a sinner."

[25] He answered and said, "Whether He is a sinner or not I do not know. One thing I know: that though I was blind, now I see."

[26] Then they said to him again, "What did He do to you? How did He open your eyes?"

[27] He answered them, "I told you already, and you did not listen. Why do you want to hear it again? Do you also want to become His disciples?"

[28] Then they reviled him and said, "You are His disciple, but we are Moses' disciples. [29] We know that God spoke to Moses; as for this fellow, we do not know where He is from."

[30] The man answered and said to them, "Why, this is a marvelous thing, that you do not know where He is from; yet He has opened my eyes! [31] Now we know that God does not hear sinners; but if anyone is a worshiper of God and does His will, He hears him. [32] Since the world began it has been unheard of that anyone opened the eyes of one who was born blind. [33] If this Man were not from God, He could do nothing."

[34] They answered and said to him, "You were completely born in sins, and are you teaching us?" And they cast him out.

[35] Jesus heard that they had cast him out; and when He had found him, He said to him, "Do you believe in the Son of God?"

[36] He answered and said, "Who is He, Lord, that I may believe in Him?"

[37] And Jesus said to him, "You have both seen Him and it is He who is talking with you."

[38] Then he said, "Lord, I believe!" And he worshiped Him.

[39] And Jesus said, "For judgment I have come into this world, that those who do not see may see, and that those who see may be made blind."

[40] Then some of the Pharisees who were with Him heard these words, and said to Him, "Are we blind also?"

[41] Jesus said to them, "If you were blind, you would have no sin; but now you say, 'We see.' Therefore your sin remains."

3. How did the people respond when the man told them about his miraculous healing (see verses 16–19)?

_____

_____

_____

4. What did Jesus do when He learned the man had been cast out of the temple? How did the man react when he realized Jesus was the One who had healed him (see verses 35–39)?

_____

_____

_____

_____

The Good Shepherd (John 10:1–15)

¹ "Most assuredly, I say to you, he who does not enter the sheepfold by the door, but climbs up some other way, the same is a thief and a robber. ² But he who enters by the door is the shepherd of the sheep. ³ To him the doorkeeper opens, and the sheep hear his voice; and he calls his own sheep by name and leads them out. ⁴ And when he brings out his own sheep, he goes before them; and the sheep follow him, for they know his voice. ⁵ Yet they will by no means follow a stranger, but will flee from him, for they do not know the voice of strangers."

⁷ Then Jesus said to them again, "Most assuredly, I say to you, I am the door of the sheep. ⁸ All who ever came before Me are thieves and robbers, but the sheep did not hear them. ⁹ I am the door. If anyone enters by Me, he will be saved, and will go in and out and find pasture. ¹⁰ The thief does not come except to steal, and to kill, and to destroy. I have come that they may have life, and that they may have it more abundantly.

¹¹ "I am the good shepherd. The good shepherd gives His life for the sheep. ¹² But a hireling, he who is not the shepherd, one who does not own the sheep, sees the wolf coming and leaves the sheep and flees; and the wolf catches the sheep and scatters them. ¹³ The hireling flees because he is a hireling and does not care about the sheep. ¹⁴ I am the good shepherd; and I know My sheep, and am known by My own. ¹⁵ As the Father knows Me, even so I know the Father; and I lay down My life for the sheep."

5. Unlike the religious leaders, who sought only to force their interpretation of God's laws on the people, Jesus came to care for them as a "good shepherd" to His flock. How does Jesus say the people will recognize that He is their true shepherd (see verses 1–5)?

6. What did Jesus say He came to bring to all who follow Him (see verse 10)?

Further Conflict Over Jesus' Claims (John 10:22–39)

²² Now it was the Feast of Dedication in Jerusalem, and it was winter. ²³ And Jesus walked in the temple, in Solomon's porch. ²⁴ Then the Jews surrounded Him and said to Him, "How long do You keep us in doubt? If You are the Christ, tell us plainly."

²⁵ Jesus answered them, "I told you, and you do not believe. The works that I do in My Father's name, they bear witness of Me. ²⁶ But you do not believe, because you are not of My sheep, as I said to you. ²⁷ My sheep hear My voice, and I know them, and they follow Me. ²⁸ And I give them eternal life, and they shall never perish; neither shall anyone snatch them out of My hand. ²⁹ My Father, who has given them to Me, is greater than all; and no one is able to snatch them out of My Father's hand. ³⁰ I and My Father are one."

³¹ Then the Jews took up stones again to stone Him. ³² Jesus answered them, "Many good works I have shown you from My Father. For which of those works do you stone Me?"

³³ The Jews answered Him, saying, "For a good work we do not stone You, but for blasphemy, and because You, being a Man, make Yourself God."

³⁴ Jesus answered them, "Is it not written in your law, 'I said, "You are gods" '? ³⁵ If He called them gods, to whom the word of God came (and the Scripture cannot be broken), ³⁶ do you say of Him whom the Father sanctified and sent into the world, 'You are blaspheming,' because I said, 'I am the Son of God'? ³⁷ If I do not do the works of My Father, do not believe Me; ³⁸ but if I do, though you do not believe Me, believe the works, that you may know and believe that the Father is in Me, and I in Him." ³⁹ Therefore they sought again to seize Him, but He escaped out of their hand.

---

7. How did Jesus respond when the Jewish leaders asked if He was the Christ? According to Jesus, why didn't they believe Him (see verses 25–30)?

_____

_____

_____

_____

_____

8. Why did the religious leaders want to kill Jesus? What test did Jesus suggest they employ to judge whether His claims were accurate (see verses 31–38)?

_____

_____

_____

_____

_____

_____

REVIEWING THE STORY

Jesus performed a number of miracles during His ministry, but the healing of the man born blind was especially profound. However, the Jewish religious leaders failed to recognize its importance. They only saw that Jesus healed on the Sabbath—which they felt went against Jewish Law—and tried to kill Him because of His claims to be God. Jesus sparred with them, but His focus was always on His followers and those who were receptive to His teachings. He truly was the Good Shepherd who cared for and protected His flock.

9. When the disciples passed by the man born blind, Jesus assured them that the man's condition was not due to anyone's sin. What surprising reason did Jesus suggest was actually the cause of the man's blindness (see John 9:1–3)?

_____

_____

_____

_____

_____

10. What reasons did the man born blind give to the religious leaders as to why he believed that Jesus had been sent from God (see John 9:30–33)?

_____

_____

_____

11. What did Jesus say was the difference between His ministry and that of the religious leaders? How did Jesus reveal that His message of salvation was not just for the Jewish people but for the entire world (see John 10:11–16)?

_____

_____

_____

12. Why do you think the Jewish religious leaders refused to even consider the possibility that Jesus was who He claimed to be (see John 10:25–30)?

_____

_____

_____

APPLYING THE MESSAGE

13. When the Pharisees tried to debate the man who had been healed by Jesus, he said, "One thing I know: that though I was blind, now I see" (John 9:25). If someone tried to debate with you over your experience with Jesus, how would you respond?

_____

_____

14. Jesus' enemies claimed that He had a demon or that He was crazy. How do opponents of Jesus try to dismiss Him today?

REFLECTING ON THE MEANING

Jesus' interactions with the man born blind reveal three timeless truths for believers today. The first of these truths is that *religion is not the best place to learn about Christ.* Religion is an attempt to reach up to God through what *we* do. Christianity is God reaching down to us through what *Christ* did on our behalf. The man born blind tried to find answers and tried to explain what happened to him in the context of religion. It didn't work.

The second truth is that *resistance is not a liability but an asset to our spiritual growth.* Coming to know Jesus Christ does not solve all of our problems or guarantee smooth sailing for the rest of our lives. After the blind man encountered Christ, he was ostracized by his neighbors and banished from the synagogue by the religious leaders. Yet through it all, he found his relationship with Christ strengthened. In the same way, if we encounter resistance because of what Jesus has done for us, we shouldn't be too quick to try to pray away our struggles. God may be strengthening our spiritual muscles and preparing us for the work He has ahead.

The third truth is that *regeneration is not a matter of having overwhelming evidence but a matter of having an encounter with Christ.* The Jewish leaders had all the evidence they needed about Jesus. Standing before them was a man born blind who could now see! Never before had such a miracle been performed. Yet no amount of proof, reasoning, or education could make them accept Christ. The blind man knew more about Jesus in an instant than the religious leaders would ever learn . . . all because he had a personal encounter with Christ.

JOURNALING YOUR RESPONSE

How will you react the next time you face opposition because of your relationship with Christ?

A PREMATURE BURIAL

John 11:1–57

GETTING STARTED

What is something that Jesus has done in your life that others cannot deny or refute?

SETTING THE STAGE

The Gospel of John is structured around seven key miracles of Christ. The first is Jesus turning water to wine (2:1–12), followed by the healing of the nobleman's son (4:46–54), the healing of the paralytic at the pool (5:1–15), the feeding of the five thousand (6:1–14), Jesus walking on water (6:15–21), and the healing of the man born blind (9:1–12). The seventh miracle, the raising of Lazarus from the dead, is the climactic miracle of the Gospels. It is arguably the most important miracle recorded in the New Testament apart from the resurrection of Jesus Christ.

The events of the story, which are recorded in John 11, take place just before the beginning of the final week of Jesus' ministry. The Jewish leaders had become increasingly worried about Jesus' influence on the people, and as a result had stepped up their efforts to put an end to His life. They were just waiting for just the right opportunity to act. Jesus knew this, yet when He received word of Lazarus's illness, He said "Let us go to Judea again" (11:7).

The raising of Lazarus is the longest recorded miracle in John's Gospel: there are forty-six verses dedicated to its story. The detail is impressive—no key point is neglected. John paints a picture in its totality that allows us to see everything that is happening as the events take place . . . including the disciples' fears that Jesus will be playing right into the Jewish leaders' hands if He makes the journey back toward Jerusalem.

As it turns out, their fears were justified. The miracle only served to increase the religious leaders' hostility toward Jesus, for He had done something that they could not refute. Many people had been present to witness the death of Lazarus, and these same people later saw him walking around the streets of Bethany. It was impossible for the religious leaders to try to refute or deny that Jesus had true miracle-working power. So after Lazarus was raised from the dead, they redoubled their efforts to put an end to Jesus' life.

EXPLORING THE TEXT

The Death of Lazarus (John 11:1–16)

¹ Now a certain man was sick, Lazarus of Bethany, the town of Mary and her sister Martha. ² It was that Mary who anointed the Lord with fragrant oil and wiped His feet with her hair, whose brother Lazarus was sick. ³ Therefore the sisters sent to Him, saying, "Lord, behold, he whom You love is sick."

⁴ When Jesus heard that, He said, "This sickness is not unto death, but for the glory of God, that the Son of God may be glorified through it."

⁵ Now Jesus loved Martha and her sister and Lazarus. ⁶ So, when He heard that he was sick, He stayed two more days in the place where He was. ⁷ Then after this He said to the disciples, "Let us go to Judea again."

⁸ The disciples said to Him, "Rabbi, lately the Jews sought to stone You, and are You going there again?"

⁹ Jesus answered, "Are there not twelve hours in the day? If anyone walks in the day, he does not stumble, because he sees the light of this world. ¹⁰ But if one walks in the night, he stumbles, because the light is not in him." ¹¹ These things He said, and after that He said to them, "Our friend Lazarus sleeps, but I go that I may wake him up."

¹² Then His disciples said, "Lord, if he sleeps he will get well." ¹³ However, Jesus spoke of his death, but they thought that He was speaking about taking rest in sleep.

¹⁴ Then Jesus said to them plainly, "Lazarus is dead. ¹⁵ And I am glad for your sakes that I was not there, that you may believe. Nevertheless let us go to him."

¹⁶ Then Thomas, who is called the Twin, said to his fellow disciples, "Let us also go, that we may die with Him."

1. Why didn't Jesus immediately go to Bethany to heal His beloved friend Lazarus? What was the reason for Jesus' delay (see verses 1–6)?

_____

_____

_____

_____

_____

2. The village of Bethany was less than two miles away from Jerusalem. What did the disciples fear would happen if Jesus agreed to Mary and Martha's request (see verses 8, 16)?

_____

_____

_____

_____

_____

Jesus Comforts Martha (John 11:17–29)

17 So when Jesus came, He found that he had already been in the tomb four days. 18 Now Bethany was near Jerusalem, about two miles away. 19 And many of the Jews had joined the women around Martha and Mary, to comfort them concerning their brother.

20 Then Martha, as soon as she heard that Jesus was coming, went and met Him, but Mary was sitting in the house. 21 Now Martha said to Jesus, "Lord, if You had been here, my brother would not have died. 22 But even now I know that whatever You ask of God, God will give You."

23 Jesus said to her, "Your brother will rise again."

24 Martha said to Him, "I know that he will rise again in the resurrection at the last day."

²⁵ Jesus said to her, "I am the resurrection and the life. He who believes in Me, though he may die, he shall live. ²⁶ And whoever lives and believes in Me shall never die. Do you believe this?"

²⁷ She said to Him, "Yes, Lord, I believe that You are the Christ, the Son of God, who is to come into the world."

²⁸ And when she had said these things, she went her way and secretly called Mary her sister, saying, "The Teacher has come and is calling for you." ²⁹ As soon as she heard that, she arose quickly and came to Him.

3. According to rabbinic tradition, the soul of a person who died hovered over the corpse for three days and then departed on the fourth day. What did Martha believe that Jesus could do in spite of this obvious and overwhelming obstacle (see verses 20–22)?

4. How did Martha misinterpret Jesus' words when He said that Lazarus would rise again? How did Jesus correct her understanding (see verses 23–26)?

Jesus Comes to the Tomb of Lazarus (John 11:30–40)

[30] Now Jesus had not yet come into the town, but was in the place where Martha met Him. [31] Then the Jews who were with her in the house, and comforting her, when they saw that Mary rose up quickly and went out, followed her, saying, "She is going to the tomb to weep there."

[32] Then, when Mary came where Jesus was, and saw Him, she fell down at His feet, saying to Him, "Lord, if You had been here, my brother would not have died."

[33] Therefore, when Jesus saw her weeping, and the Jews who came with her weeping, He groaned in the spirit and was troubled. [34] And He said, "Where have you laid him?"

They said to Him, "Lord, come and see."

[35] Jesus wept. [36] Then the Jews said, "See how He loved him!"

[37] And some of them said, "Could not this Man, who opened the eyes of the blind, also have kept this man from dying?"

[38] Then Jesus, again groaning in Himself, came to the tomb. It was a cave, and a stone lay against it. [39] Jesus said, "Take away the stone."

Martha, the sister of him who was dead, said to Him, "Lord, by this time there is a stench, for he has been dead four days."

[40] Jesus said to her, "Did I not say to you that if you would believe you would see the glory of God?"

---

5. How did Mary react when she saw Jesus? What similarities and differences were there between her response and that of Martha (see verses 31–32)?

_____

_____

_____

_____

6. How did Jesus demonstrate in this passage that He can relate to the suffering that we face in this world (see verses 33–36)?

_____

_____

_____

_____

_____

_____

_____

Jesus Raises Lazarus from the Dead (John 11:41–52)

⁴¹ Then they took away the stone from the place where the dead man was lying. And Jesus lifted up His eyes and said, "Father, I thank You that You have heard Me. ⁴² And I know that You always hear Me, but because of the people who are standing by I said this, that they may believe that You sent Me." ⁴³ Now when He had said these things, He cried with a loud voice, "Lazarus, come forth!" ⁴⁴ And he who had died came out bound hand and foot with graveclothes, and his face was wrapped with a cloth. Jesus said to them, "Loose him, and let him go."

⁴⁵ Then many of the Jews who had come to Mary, and had seen the things Jesus did, believed in Him. ⁴⁶ But some of them went away to the Pharisees and told them the things Jesus did. ⁴⁷ Then the chief priests and the Pharisees gathered a council and said, "What shall we do? For this Man works many signs. ⁴⁸ If we let Him alone like this, everyone will believe in Him, and the Romans will come and take away both our place and nation."

⁴⁹ And one of them, Caiaphas, being high priest that year, said to them, "You know nothing at all, ⁵⁰ nor do you consider that it is expedient for us that one man should die for the people, and not that the whole nation should perish." ⁵¹ Now this he did not say on

his own authority; but being high priest that year he prophesied that Jesus would die for the nation, [52] and not for that nation only, but also that He would gather together in one the children of God who were scattered abroad.

---

7. What did Jesus do before calling Lazarus to come out of the tomb? What did He indicate was the reason He was performing this miracle (see verses 41–42)?

_____

_____

_____

_____

_____

_____

_____

_____

8. What was the people's reaction to this miracle? Why was Jesus an especially vexing problem for the chief priests and Pharisees (see verses 45–48)?

_____

_____

_____

_____

_____

_____

_____

_____

REVIEWING THE STORY

The disciples had seen Jesus perform many miracles during their time with Him on earth. They had witnessed Him raise a widow's son in Nain (see Luke 7:11–17) and the daughter of a man named Jairus (see Mark 5:21–24, 35–43). But the Gospels record no instance of Jesus raising someone who had been dead for *four* days. In spite of this, when Jesus met Martha outside the village of Bethany, she confessed her belief that God would give Jesus *whatever* he asked. However, when Jesus said her brother would indeed rise again, she immediately assumed He was referring to Lazarus's resurrection "at the last day" (John 11:24). Jesus corrected this misunderstanding by demonstrating His power over death in the *present*. The raising of Lazarus stunned the Pharisees, who quickly accelerated their plans to put Jesus to death.

9. Jesus knew that Lazarus had died before He and the disciples reached Bethany. Why did Jesus say He was glad He was not there to witness it (see John 11:12–15)?

_____

_____

_____

_____

_____

10. How did Martha respond when she learned that Jesus had finally arrived in Bethany? How did she demonstrate she had complete faith in Christ (see John 11:20–27)?

_____

_____

_____

_____

_____

11. How did the people of Bethany react when Jesus arrived (see John 11:33–37)?

_____

_____

_____

_____

_____

_____

12. Caiaphas, the high priest, believed it was better to kill Jesus than allow the entire nation to continue to be "deceived" by Him . . . in spite of the consequences. How does John say these words proved to be more prophetic than Caiaphas imagined (see John 11:49–52)?

_____

_____

_____

_____

_____

APPLYING THE MESSAGE

13. Jesus told Martha that He was "the resurrection and the life" (John 11:25). What do these words mean for you in your life?

_____

_____

_____

_____

_____

14. Martha and Mary underestimated Jesus. What are some ways you have been guilty of the same? How can you avoid underestimating what Jesus is capable of doing?

_____

_____

_____

_____

_____

REFLECTING ON THE MEANING

Jesus approached Lazarus's tomb and said, "Take away the stone." Martha's reply was telling. She said, "Lord, by this time there is a stench, for he has been dead four days" (John 11:39). Martha didn't believe. She was struggling with her doubts. She did not fully understand the Lord's power . . . or His timetable.

Jesus had explained that He *could* raise Lazarus from the dead. And Martha had offered a theologically sound response to His words: "I know that he will rise again in the resurrection at the last day" (verse 24). Martha had an impressive knowledge of what the Lord would accomplish—at some point in the future. But she had no expectation that her brother, who had been in the tomb now for four days, was about to walk alive.

Isn't it interesting that this godly woman, who had Christ by her side, was preoccupied with her brother's corpse? The Son of God had made Himself available to her, yet she could only think about her problem. Granted, her problem was enormous, but the power by her side was even greater.

Many Christians share Martha's preoccupation. While Jesus does not physically stand by our side, we have something better. We have His Holy Spirit dwelling within us. Like Martha, we have His power available to us. But often when problems come, like Martha we allow them to fill our vision and block out everything there is to know about Christ. Instead of focusing on the enormity of His power and His love for us, we focus on the enormity of the problem before us. We see no apparent solution, no reason for hope . . . and so we assume there is none.

Yet if Martha's experience at her brother's tomb teaches us anything, it is that where Jesus is, there is hope.

JOURNALING YOUR RESPONSE

What particular problems tend to block your view of Jesus' mercy and power?

TREACHEROUS TIMES
John 12:1–13:38

GETTING STARTED

What is the most devastating betrayal you have experienced? How did it affect you?

_____

_____

_____

_____

_____

_____

_____

_____

_____

_____

SETTING THE STAGE

Jesus' raising of Lazarus from the dead serves as the catalyst for the events that will soon transpire during what is known as "Passion Week"—arguably the most momentous week in history. It begins with Jesus' arrival in the village of Bethany at the request of Mary and Martha, who have summoned Jesus to come and heal their brother. It will end with the treachery of the Jewish religious leaders, a betrayal from one of Jesus' own disciples, and a Roman cross.

The apostle John devotes nearly half of his Gospel to the events of this one week—which include Jesus' anointing at Bethany, His triumphal entry into Jerusalem, His cursing of the fig tree, the Olivet discourse, His final teachings, the Last Supper, His arrest and trials, and His crucifixion. Three days after His burial, the events of the week climax in Jesus' resurrection.

In John's Gospel, the week begins with a supper Jesus is attending in Bethany. It is during this meal that Mary, the sister of Martha and Lazarus, anoints Jesus with an expensive and fragrant oil extracted from the nard plant, which grew in the mountains of northern India. The supper was held in the house of Simon the leper, no doubt a man whom Jesus had healed of leprosy. The meal's likely purpose was to celebrate the raising of Lazarus from the dead.

It was a brave thing for the friends of Jesus to attend that dinner. The Sanhedrin (the Jewish high court) had given an order that anyone who knew Jesus' location was to report it to the authorities. Failure to do so would make a person an accomplice of Jesus in what the Jewish religious leaders considered to be His crimes.

Still, Jesus' friends openly dined with Him in Simon's home. As a result, at least one of them faced danger.

EXPLORING THE TEXT

Anointing and Triumphal Entry (John 12:1–16)

1 Then, six days before the Passover, Jesus came to Bethany, where Lazarus was who had been dead, whom He had raised from the dead. 2 There they made Him a supper; and Martha served, but Lazarus was one of those who sat at the table with Him. 3 Then Mary took a pound of very costly oil of spikenard, anointed the feet of Jesus, and wiped His feet with her hair. And the house was filled with the fragrance of the oil.

⁴ But one of His disciples, Judas Iscariot, Simon's son, who would betray Him, said, ⁵ "Why was this fragrant oil not sold for three hundred denarii and given to the poor?" ⁶ This he said, not that he cared for the poor, but because he was a thief, and had the money box; and he used to take what was put in it.

⁷ But Jesus said, "Let her alone; she has kept this for the day of My burial. ⁸ For the poor you have with you always, but Me you do not have always."

⁹ Now a great many of the Jews knew that He was there; and they came, not for Jesus' sake only, but that they might also see Lazarus, whom He had raised from the dead. ¹⁰ But the chief priests plotted to put Lazarus to death also, ¹¹ because on account of him many of the Jews went away and believed in Jesus.

¹² The next day a great multitude that had come to the feast, when they heard that Jesus was coming to Jerusalem, ¹³ took branches of palm trees and went out to meet Him, and cried out:

"Hosanna!
'Blessed is He who comes in the name of the Lord!'
The King of Israel!"

¹⁴ Then Jesus, when He had found a young donkey, sat on it; as it is written:

¹⁵ "Fear not, daughter of Zion;
Behold, your King is coming,
Sitting on a donkey's colt."

¹⁶ His disciples did not understand these things at first; but when Jesus was glorified, then they remembered that these things were written about Him and that they had done these things to Him.

1. Mary anointed Jesus as an act of devotion to her Lord. How did Jesus interpret her actions following Judas's critical response (see verses 4–8)?

2. In ancient times, leaders rode horses if they were going off to war, but donkeys if they were embarking on a mission of peace. How did Jesus' choice of transport indicate the kind of mission He was undertaking? How did His actions fulfill the prophecy in Zechariah 9:9–13?

Jesus Predicts His Death (John 12:20–36)

20 Now there were certain Greeks among those who came up to worship at the feast. 21 Then they came to Philip, who was from Bethsaida of Galilee, and asked him, saying, "Sir, we wish to see Jesus."

22 Philip came and told Andrew, and in turn Andrew and Philip told Jesus.

23 But Jesus answered them, saying, "The hour has come that the Son of Man should be glorified. 24 Most assuredly, I say to you, unless a grain of wheat falls into the ground and dies, it remains alone; but if it dies, it produces much grain. 25 He who loves his life will lose it, and he who hates his life in this world will keep it for eternal life.

26 If anyone serves Me, let him follow Me; and where I am, there My servant will be also. If anyone serves Me, him My Father will honor."

27 "Now My soul is troubled, and what shall I say? 'Father, save Me from this hour'? But for this purpose I came to this hour. 28 Father, glorify Your name."

Then a voice came from heaven, saying, "I have both glorified it and will glorify it again."

29 The crowd that was there and heard it said it had thundered; others said an angel had spoken to him.

30 Jesus said, "This voice was for your benefit, not mine. 31 Now is the time for judgment on this world; now the prince of this world will be driven out. 32 And I, when I am lifted up from the earth, will draw all people to myself." 33 He said this to show the kind of death he was going to die.

34 The crowd spoke up, "We have heard from the Law that the Messiah will remain forever, so how can you say, 'The Son of Man must be lifted up'? Who is this 'Son of Man'?"

35 Then Jesus told them, "You are going to have the light just a little while longer. Walk while you have the light, before darkness overtakes you. Whoever walks in the dark does not know where they are going. 36 Believe in the light while you have the light, so that you may become children of light." When he had finished speaking, Jesus left and hid himself from them.

---

3. What did Jesus say to Andrew and Philip about the "hour" that had now arrived? What was He saying to them about the purpose of His coming sacrifice (see verses 23–27)?

4. Why was the voice from God the people heard for their benefit? What did Jesus say would soon come to pass (see verses 30–32, 35–36)?

_____

_____

_____

_____

_____

Jesus Washes the Disciples' Feet (John 13:1–17)

¹ Now before the Feast of the Passover, when Jesus knew that His hour had come that He should depart from this world to the Father, having loved His own who were in the world, He loved them to the end.

² And supper being ended, the devil having already put it into the heart of Judas Iscariot, Simon's son, to betray Him, ³ Jesus, knowing that the Father had given all things into His hands, and that He had come from God and was going to God, ⁴ rose from supper and laid aside His garments, took a towel and girded Himself. ⁵ After that, He poured water into a basin and began to wash the disciples' feet, and to wipe them with the towel with which He was girded. ⁶ Then He came to Simon Peter. And Peter said to Him, "Lord, are You washing my feet?"

⁷ Jesus answered and said to him, "What I am doing you do not understand now, but you will know after this."

⁸ Peter said to Him, "You shall never wash my feet!"

Jesus answered him, "If I do not wash you, you have no part with Me."

⁹ Simon Peter said to Him, "Lord, not my feet only, but also my hands and my head!"

¹⁰ Jesus said to him, "He who is bathed needs only to wash his feet, but is completely clean; and you are clean, but not all of you."

¹¹ For He knew who would betray Him; therefore He said, "You are not all clean."

¹² So when He had washed their feet, taken His garments, and sat down again, He said to them, "Do you know what I have done to you? ¹³ You call Me Teacher and Lord, and you say well, for so I am. ¹⁴ If I then, your Lord and Teacher, have washed your feet, you also ought to wash one another's feet. ¹⁵ For I have given you an example, that you should do as I have done to you. ¹⁶ Most assuredly, I say to you, a servant is not greater than his master; nor is he who is sent greater than he who sent him. ¹⁷ If you know these things, blessed are you if you do them."

---

5. The act of washing a guest's feet was a common courtesy in Jesus' day but was typically only something the lowest of servants performed. Why were Jesus' actions striking in this regard? Why didn't Peter understand what Jesus was doing (see verses 2–7)?

_____

_____

_____

_____

_____

6. How did Jesus respond when Peter protested the foot washing? What do you think Jesus meant by these words (see verses 7–10)?

_____

_____

_____

_____

_____

The New Commandment (John 13:21–38)

[21] When Jesus had said these things, He was troubled in spirit, and testified and said, "Most assuredly, I say to you, one of you will betray Me." [22] Then the disciples looked at one another, perplexed about whom He spoke.

[23] Now there was leaning on Jesus' bosom one of His disciples, whom Jesus loved. [24] Simon Peter therefore motioned to him to ask who it was of whom He spoke.

[25] Then, leaning back on Jesus' breast, he said to Him, "Lord, who is it?"

[26] Jesus answered, "It is he to whom I shall give a piece of bread when I have dipped it." And having dipped the bread, He gave it to Judas Iscariot, the son of Simon. [27] Now after the piece of bread, Satan entered him. Then Jesus said to him, "What you do, do quickly." [28] But no one at the table knew for what reason He said this to him. [29] For some thought, because Judas had the money box, that Jesus had said to him, "Buy those things we need for the feast," or that he should give something to the poor.

[30] Having received the piece of bread, he then went out immediately. And it was night.

[31] So, when he had gone out, Jesus said, "Now the Son of Man is glorified, and God is glorified in Him. [32] If God is glorified in Him, God will also glorify Him in Himself, and glorify Him immediately. [33] Little children, I shall be with you a little while longer. You will seek Me; and as I said to the Jews, 'Where I am going, you cannot come,' so now I say to you. [34] A new commandment I give to you, that you love one another; as I have loved you, that you also love one another. [35] By this all will know that you are My disciples, if you have love for one another."

[36] Simon Peter said to Him, "Lord, where are You going?"

Jesus answered him, "Where I am going you cannot follow Me now, but you shall follow Me afterward."

³⁷ Peter said to Him, "Lord, why can I not follow You now? I will lay down my life for Your sake."

³⁸ Jesus answered him, "Will you lay down your life for My sake? Most assuredly, I say to you, the rooster shall not crow till you have denied Me three times."

---

7. How did Jesus indicate He knew that Judas would betray Him? How did the disciples misunderstand His action of singling out this betrayer (see verses 26–29)?

8. Read Leviticus 19:18. What made the instructions Jesus was giving to His disciples to love one another a "new" command (see verses 34–35)?

REVIEWING THE STORY

Treachery was afoot as Jesus made His way to Jerusalem for the final week of His life. His enemies plotted to kill not just Him but also those associated with Him like Lazarus, who drew attention to Christ. Jesus predicted His enemies would crucify Him. He also predicted Judas Iscariot would betray Him and Simon Peter would deny Him. With so much treachery—from both the inside and outside—Jesus' faithful followers needed a support system. Thus, Jesus gave them a new commandment: love one another as He had loved them.

9. What were the two contrasting attitudes toward Jesus as He entered Jerusalem for the Passover celebration (see John 12:9–13)?

_____

_____

_____

_____

10. What did Jesus tell the crowds who came to see Him what they needed to do while He was still present with them (see John 12:35–36)?

_____

_____

_____

_____

11. What did Jesus say was the purpose of His washing of the disciples' feet? What lessons did He want them to take from it (see John 13:12–17)?

_____

_____

_____

12. Jesus set a high standard when He told His disciples to love "as I have loved you" (John 13:34). What does it mean for Jesus' followers to love others the way He loved?

APPLYING THE MESSAGE

13. The spikenard Mary used to anoint Jesus would have cost the equivalent of a year's wages for an average worker. What is the most significant and meaningful sacrifice that you have made for Jesus' sake?

14. When faced with difficulties, why is it so tempting to pray, "Father, save me from this hour"? Why is it more important to pray, "Father, glorify Your name" (John 12:27–28)?

REFLECTING ON THE MEANING

The crowd that welcomed Jesus to Jerusalem did so with a seemingly worshipful attitude. Yet while the multitudes went through the right motions, said the right things, and sang the right songs, the events of the crucifixion that would soon take place reveal that their worship was not genuine. The key to genuine worship is *preparation*.

There are four actions God's people can take to prepare for worship. The first is to *come with a sincere heart*. Acceptable worship requires a heart that is fixed on God and His glory. Double-mindedness, preoccupation with self, and preoccupation with the world are obstacles to sincere worship. The way you live, pray, and study the Bible will all impact your worship. If your heart is fixed on God throughout the week, it will show in your worship.

The second action is to *come in faith*. If you have confidence in your relationship with God, you will be able to worship Him in a way that pleases Him and refreshes you. So, if you sense there's something in your life that's keeping you from placing your absolute confidence in God, pray about it and take the necessary steps to remove the obstacle before you worship.

The third action is to *come in humility*. You do this by meditating on the undeserved favor you have received from God. You do it by recognizing the Lord's majesty and your own unworthiness. You open yourself to Him with a sincere amazement and celebration of who God is and what He has done.

The fourth action is to *come in daily purity*. In Hebrews 10:22, we read, "Let us draw near . . . with our bodies washed with pure water." The way to do this is to come clean before God—to confess the sin you know about and sincerely seek His forgiveness. Then ask God to enable you in your worship experience to lift up holy hands to Him.

Journaling Your Response

What steps can you take to make your worship more impactful and meaningful?

_____

_____

_____

_____

_____

_____

_____

_____

LESSON *eight*

THE TRUE VINE
John 14:1–15:27

GETTING STARTED

Have you ever had someone ask if you were a Christian based on something you said, did, or refused to do? If so, how did that make you feel?

_____

_____

_____

_____

_____

_____

_____

_____

_____

_____

_____

_____

_____

_____

_____

_____

_____

SETTING THE STAGE

The disciples were troubled and discouraged because Jesus had told them that He would soon leave them. Jesus revealed to them that this would involve His death. Even worse, He also dropped the bombshell that one of His disciples would betray Him. Those words had barely sunk in when Jesus broke the news to Peter, the rock-solid leader of the disciples, that he would deny even knowing Jesus three times.

The final blow came when Jesus told His disciples that *every one of them* would forsake Him. "Jesus said to them, 'All of you will be made to stumble because of Me this night, for it is written: "I will strike the Shepherd, and the sheep of the flock will be scattered" ' " (Matthew 26:31). His trusted companions would abandon Him when He needed them most.

Imagine for a moment the impact of all this news coming within a few short hours. You can understand why the disciples must have been in a state of depression, shock, and even denial. Added to this was the fact that the disciples saw Jesus troubled, but they could not comprehend the reason for His distress. Surely, though, they were alarmed by the change in Jesus' demeanor. Surely they could sense the spiritual ground shifting below their feet.

The disciples faced a situation that was intensely discouraging. But into that setting—in spite of what Jesus knew was to come—He spoke words to His disciples to encourage them and lift them up. These words could not have been more appropriate, given the circumstances. He looked at His disciples and said, "Let not your heart be troubled" (John 14:1).

EXPLORING THE TEXT

Jesus Comforts His Disciples (John 14:1–14)

> [1] "Let not your heart be troubled; you believe in God, believe also in Me. [2] In My Father's house are many mansions; if it were not so, I would have told you. I go to prepare a place for you. [3] And if I go

and prepare a place for you, I will come again and receive you to Myself; that where I am, there you may be also. ⁴ And where I go you know, and the way you know."

⁵ Thomas said to Him, "Lord, we do not know where You are going, and how can we know the way?"

⁶ Jesus said to him, "I am the way, the truth, and the life. No one comes to the Father except through Me.

⁷ "If you had known Me, you would have known My Father also; and from now on you know Him and have seen Him."

⁸ Philip said to Him, "Lord, show us the Father, and it is sufficient for us."

⁹ Jesus said to him, "Have I been with you so long, and yet you have not known Me, Philip? He who has seen Me has seen the Father; so how can you say, 'Show us the Father'? ¹⁰ Do you not believe that I am in the Father, and the Father in Me? The words that I speak to you I do not speak on My own authority; but the Father who dwells in Me does the works. ¹¹ Believe Me that I am in the Father and the Father in Me, or else believe Me for the sake of the works themselves.

¹² "Most assuredly, I say to you, he who believes in Me, the works that I do he will do also; and greater works than these he will do, because I go to My Father. ¹³ And whatever you ask in My name, that I will do, that the Father may be glorified in the Son. ¹⁴ If you ask anything in My name, I will do it."

---

1. What are some of the promises that Jesus made to His disciples (see verses 1–3, 12–14)?

2. Philip asked Jesus to show them the Father—in spite of the many miracles he had already seen Jesus perform. How did Jesus respond to his request (see verses 9–11)?

_____

_____

_____

_____

_____

_____

Jesus Promises Another Helper (John 14:15–31)

15 "If you love Me, keep My commandments. 16 And I will pray the Father, and He will give you another Helper, that He may abide with you forever— 17 the Spirit of truth, whom the world cannot receive, because it neither sees Him nor knows Him; but you know Him, for He dwells with you and will be in you. 18 I will not leave you orphans; I will come to you.

19 "A little while longer and the world will see Me no more, but you will see Me. Because I live, you will live also. 20 At that day you will know that I am in My Father, and you in Me, and I in you. 21 He who has My commandments and keeps them, it is he who loves Me. And he who loves Me will be loved by My Father, and I will love him and manifest Myself to him."

22 Judas (not Iscariot) said to Him, "Lord, how is it that You will manifest Yourself to us, and not to the world?"

23 Jesus answered and said to him, "If anyone loves Me, he will keep My word; and My Father will love him, and We will come to him and make Our home with him. 24 He who does not love Me does not keep My words; and the word which you hear is not Mine but the Father's who sent Me.

25 "These things I have spoken to you while being present with you. 26 But the Helper, the Holy Spirit, whom the Father will send in My name, He will teach you all things, and bring to your remembrance all things that I said to you. 27 Peace I leave with you, My peace I give to you; not as the world gives do I give to you. Let not your heart be troubled, neither let it be afraid. 28 You have heard Me say to you, 'I am going away and coming back to you.' If you loved Me, you would rejoice because I said, 'I am going to the Father,' for My Father is greater than I.

29 "And now I have told you before it comes, that when it does come to pass, you may believe. 30 I will no longer talk much with you, for the ruler of this world is coming, and he has nothing in Me. 31 But that the world may know that I love the Father, and as the Father gave Me commandment, so I do. Arise, let us go from here."

---

3. What connection did Jesus make between loving Him and keeping His commands? What promise did He make to those who love Him (see verses 15–23)?

4. Why did Jesus say the disciples should rejoice that He was going away (see verses 28–31)?

The Vine and the Branches (John 15:1–17)

[1] "I am the true vine, and My Father is the vinedresser. [2] Every branch in Me that does not bear fruit He takes away; and every branch that bears fruit He prunes, that it may bear more fruit. [3] You are already clean because of the word which I have spoken to you. [4] Abide in Me, and I in you. As the branch cannot bear fruit of itself, unless it abides in the vine, neither can you, unless you abide in Me.

[5] "I am the vine, you are the branches. He who abides in Me, and I in him, bears much fruit; for without Me you can do nothing. [6] If anyone does not abide in Me, he is cast out as a branch and is withered; and they gather them and throw them into the fire, and they are burned. [7] If you abide in Me, and My words abide in you, you will ask what you desire, and it shall be done for you. [8] By this My Father is glorified, that you bear much fruit; so you will be My disciples.

[9] "As the Father loved Me, I also have loved you; abide in My love. [10] If you keep My commandments, you will abide in My love, just as I have kept My Father's commandments and abide in His love.

[11] "These things I have spoken to you, that My joy may remain in you, and that your joy may be full. [12] This is My commandment, that you love one another as I have loved you. [13] Greater love has no one than this, than to lay down one's life for his friends. [14] You are My friends if you do whatever I command you. [15] No longer do I call you servants, for a servant does not know what his master is doing; but I have called you friends, for all things that I heard from My Father I have made known to you. [16] You did not choose Me, but I chose you and appointed you that you should go and bear fruit, and that your fruit should remain, that whatever you ask the Father in My name He may give you. [17] These things I command you, that you love one another."

5. According to Jesus, what is the importance of us (the branches) abiding in Him (the Vine)? What happens to those who do not abide in Him (see verses 1–8)?

_____

_____

_____

_____

_____

_____

6. What is the difference between being Jesus' servant and His friend (see verses 13–15)?

_____

_____

_____

_____

_____

_____

_____

The World's Hatred (John 15:18–27)

18 "If the world hates you, you know that it hated Me before it hated you. 19 If you were of the world, the world would love its own. Yet because you are not of the world, but I chose you out of the world, therefore the world hates you. 20 Remember the word that I said to you, 'A servant is not greater than his master.' If they persecuted Me, they will also persecute you. If they kept My word, they will keep yours also. 21 But all these things they will do to you for My name's sake, because they do not know Him who sent Me. 22 If I had not come

and spoken to them, they would have no sin, but now they have no excuse for their sin. ²³ He who hates Me hates My Father also. ²⁴ If I had not done among them the works which no one else did, they would have no sin; but now they have seen and also hated both Me and My Father. ²⁵ But this happened that the word might be fulfilled which is written in their law, 'They hated Me without a cause.'

²⁶ "But when the Helper comes, whom I shall send to you from the Father, the Spirit of truth who proceeds from the Father, He will testify of Me. ²⁷ And you also will bear witness, because you have been with Me from the beginning."

---

7. Why did Jesus say the disciples would likely be hated or persecuted (see verses 18–19)?

_____

_____

_____

_____

_____

8. Jesus emphasized that those who persecuted Him and His disciples had "no excuse for their sin." What had these people done that sealed their guilt (see verses 20–25)?

_____

_____

_____

_____

_____

_____

REVIEWING THE STORY

Jesus presented His followers with some of His most challenging teachings on the night before His crucifixion. He told them He was *the* way, *the* truth and *the* life, which meant that any other way—including those followed by the pagans and the Jewish religious leaders—was not true or valid. Only branches connected to the true Vine (Jesus) could bear genuine fruit. Understandably, such a position would cause bitterness and opposition for those who did not accept it. Thus, Jesus warned His followers to expect to be hated . . . just as He was hated.

9. Compare Proverbs 14:12 with John 14:6. Why do you think "other ways" to get to heaven seem right to some people? What is the end result for those who trust in those ways?

_____

_____

_____

_____

_____

_____

10. What promise did Jesus make about how the Holy Spirit would help those who believe in Him (see John 14:25–28)?

_____

_____

_____

_____

_____

_____

11. What kind of spiritual fruit do you think would be evident from a branch that abides in the true Vine (see John 15:1–8)? How can you abide in the Vine (see verses 9–10)?

_____

_____

_____

_____

_____

12. Why is the amount of spiritual persecution or opposition a disciple faces a good way to measure the person's effectiveness as a servant of Christ (see John 15:18–20)?

_____

_____

_____

_____

APPLYING THE MESSAGE

13. If you were talking with a spiritual seeker who believes there are many different paths to God, how would you share the truth of John 14:6 in a loving way?

_____

_____

_____

_____

_____

14. Pruning, in the spiritual sense, involves cutting away unproductive areas of a disciple's life. This is rarely a pleasant process, but why is it so important to a disciple's spiritual growth?

_____

_____

_____

_____

REFLECTING ON THE MEANING

The disciples were troubled by the news that soon Jesus would no longer be with them. So Jesus gave them—and us—three dynamic principles for overcoming a troubled spirit. First, Jesus reminds us that we have a *Person* to whom we can always appeal. He says, in effect, "I know that as Jews, you believe in God. So just as you believe in Him, believe in Me, for I am God in the flesh." In every set of difficult circumstances, we have to decide whether we will to put our faith in Christ. If we do, He will not fail us.

Second, Jesus reminds us that we have a *place*. The basic desire of every human heart is to have a place we can call home—a place where we belong. For the followers of Jesus, that place is heaven. In the New Testament, heaven is called a country because it's vast. It's called a city because it's inhabited. It's called a kingdom because it's a place of order.

But when Jesus calls it His Father's house, it reminds us that it's a place where we can know the joy we feel when we gather around the table with loved ones at home. It's a place of laughter without tears, life without death, singing without mourning, contentment without crying, and pleasure without pain. Our Lord and Savior, Jesus Christ, is in that place. Our loving heavenly Father is in that place. The blessed Holy Spirit is in that place.

Third, Jesus reminds us that we have been given *promises*. There are more than enough promises in the Word of God to fill our study time for a lifetime. But one of the greatest promises is Jesus' assurance that He will be coming again.

JOURNALING YOUR RESPONSE

What are some of the ways that you have received God's perfect peace in your life?

THE PRAYERS OF JESUS
John 16:1–17:26

GETTING STARTED

On an average day, how much time do you spend with God in prayer?

SETTING THE STAGE

According the Gospel of Matthew, before Jesus inaugurated His public ministry, He went into the wilderness and spent a concerted period in prayer (see 4:1–11). He bathed His ministry in prayer before He started. Luke reports in his Gospel that before Jesus chose the twelve disciples who would walk with Him, He prayed all night (see 6:12). Mark states that in the early days of Jesus' ministry, He would rise before sunrise and find a solitary place to pray (see 1:35).

It is estimated there are some 650 prayers recorded in the Bible, given by figures such as Abraham, Moses, Joshua, Gideon, Hannah, David, Elijah, and Nehemiah. Jesus is described as praying on at least *nineteen* different occasions. One time, He taught His disciples to pray (see Matthew 6:5–13). Believers still quote the words Jesus used in that short instructional—what we call today the "Lord's Prayer" (though, more accurately, it should be called the "Disciple's Prayer," for Jesus had no reason to ask God to forgive His trespasses).

Yet there is only one prayer that reveals, in exquisite detail, what Jesus Himself said when He talked to His heavenly Father. Under the inspiration of the Holy Spirit, the apostle John recorded this entire prayer that Jesus offered in the upper room on the night He was arrested. In the span of a single chapter, John records how Jesus prayed for Himself, for His disciples, and for all believers (see John 17).

Jesus' words comprise what many Bible scholars believe to be the most important chapter in the Bible.

EXPLORING THE TEXT

Jesus Warns and Comforts His Disciples (John 16:1–16)

[1] "These things I have spoken to you, that you should not be made to stumble. [2] They will put you out of the synagogues; yes, the time is coming that whoever kills you will think that he offers God service.

³ And these things they will do to you because they have not known the Father nor Me. ⁴ But these things I have told you, that when the time comes, you may remember that I told you of them.

"And these things I did not say to you at the beginning, because I was with you.

⁵ "But now I go away to Him who sent Me, and none of you asks Me, 'Where are You going?' ⁶ But because I have said these things to you, sorrow has filled your heart. ⁷ Nevertheless I tell you the truth. It is to your advantage that I go away; for if I do not go away, the Helper will not come to you; but if I depart, I will send Him to you. ⁸ And when He has come, He will convict the world of sin, and of righteousness, and of judgment: ⁹ of sin, because they do not believe in Me; ¹⁰ of righteousness, because I go to My Father and you see Me no more; ¹¹ of judgment, because the ruler of this world is judged.

¹² "I still have many things to say to you, but you cannot bear them now. ¹³ However, when He, the Spirit of truth, has come, He will guide you into all truth; for He will not speak on His own authority, but whatever He hears He will speak; and He will tell you things to come. ¹⁴ He will glorify Me, for He will take of what is Mine and declare it to you. ¹⁵ All things that the Father has are Mine. Therefore I said that He will take of Mine and declare it to you.

¹⁶ "A little while, and you will not see Me; and again a little while, and you will see Me, because I go to the Father."

---

1. What did Jesus warn His disciples that they could expect if they continued to follow Him (see verses 1–4)?

_____

_____

_____

_____

_____

_____

2. Why did Jesus say it was to the disciples' advantage that He was going away? What would the promised Holy Spirit do when He arrived (see verses 5–11)?

Sorrow Will Turn to Joy (John 16:17–28)

¹⁷ Then some of His disciples said among themselves, "What is this that He says to us, 'A little while, and you will not see Me; and again a little while, and you will see Me'; and, 'because I go to the Father'?" ¹⁸ They said therefore, "What is this that He says, 'A little while'? We do not know what He is saying."

¹⁹ Now Jesus knew that they desired to ask Him, and He said to them, "Are you inquiring among yourselves about what I said, 'A little while, and you will not see Me; and again a little while, and you will see Me'? ²⁰ Most assuredly, I say to you that you will weep and lament, but the world will rejoice; and you will be sorrowful, but your sorrow will be turned into joy. ²¹ A woman, when she is in labor, has sorrow because her hour has come; but as soon as she has given birth to the child, she no longer remembers the anguish, for joy that a human being has been born into the world. ²² Therefore you now have sorrow; but I will see you again and your heart will rejoice, and your joy no one will take from you.

²³ "And in that day you will ask Me nothing. Most assuredly, I say to you, whatever you ask the Father in My name He will give you. ²⁴ Until now you have asked nothing in My name. Ask, and you will receive, that your joy may be full.

²⁵ "These things I have spoken to you in figurative language; but the time is coming when I will no longer speak to you in figurative

language, but I will tell you plainly about the Father. [26] In that day you will ask in My name, and I do not say to you that I shall pray the Father for you; [27] for the Father Himself loves you, because you have loved Me, and have believed that I came forth from God. [28] I came forth from the Father and have come into the world. Again, I leave the world and go to the Father."

---

3. What words from Jesus caused the disciples to murmur among themselves? What were they having difficulty understanding (see verses 17–18)?

4. How did Jesus use the metaphor of a woman in labor to describe the disciples' coming sorrow? How was He encouraging them to persevere (see verses 20–22)?

Jesus Prays for Himself and the Disciples (John 17:1–19)

¹ Jesus spoke these words, lifted up His eyes to heaven, and said: "Father, the hour has come. Glorify Your Son, that Your Son also may glorify You, ² as You have given Him authority over all flesh, that He should give eternal life to as many as You have given Him. ³ And this is eternal life, that they may know You, the only true God, and Jesus Christ whom You have sent. ⁴ I have glorified You on the earth. I have finished the work which You have given Me to do. ⁵ And now, O Father, glorify Me together with Yourself, with the glory which I had with You before the world was.

⁶ "I have manifested Your name to the men whom You have given Me out of the world. They were Yours, You gave them to Me, and they have kept Your word.⁷ Now they have known that all things which You have given Me are from You.⁸ For I have given to them the words which You have given Me; and they have received them, and have known surely that I came forth from You; and they have believed that You sent Me.

⁹ "I pray for them. I do not pray for the world but for those whom You have given Me, for they are Yours. ¹⁰ And all Mine are Yours, and Yours are Mine, and I am glorified in them. ¹¹ Now I am no longer in the world, but these are in the world, and I come to You. Holy Father, keep through Your name those whom You have given Me, that they may be one as We are. ¹² While I was with them in the world, I kept them in Your name. Those whom You gave Me I have kept; and none of them is lost except the son of perdition, that the Scripture might be fulfilled.¹³ But now I come to You, and these things I speak in the world, that they may have My joy fulfilled in themselves. ¹⁴ I have given them Your word; and the world has hated them because they are not of the world, just as I am not of the world.¹⁵ I do not pray that You should take them out of the world, but that You should keep them from the evil one. ¹⁶ They are not of the world, just as I am not of the world. ¹⁷ Sanctify them by Your truth. Your word is truth. ¹⁸ As You

sent Me into the world, I also have sent them into the world. [19] And for their sakes I sanctify Myself, that they also may be sanctified by the truth."

---

5. How did Jesus define eternal life? To whom would Jesus give eternal life (see verses 1–5)?

_____

_____

_____

_____

_____

6. Abraham interceded on behalf of Lot and the people of Sodom and Gomorrah (see Genesis 18). Moses interceded for the entire Hebrew nation (see Exodus 32). For whom did Jesus intercede? What did He ask God to do for them (see John 17:9–19)?

_____

_____

_____

_____

_____

Jesus Prays for All Believers (John 17:20–26)

[20] "I do not pray for these alone, but also for those who will believe in Me through their word; [21] that they all may be one, as You, Father, are in Me, and I in You; that they also may be one in Us, that the world may believe that You sent Me. [22] And the glory which You gave

Me I have given them, that they may be one just as We are one: [23] I in them, and You in Me; that they may be made perfect in one, and that the world may know that You have sent Me, and have loved them as You have loved Me.

[24] "Father, I desire that they also whom You gave Me may be with Me where I am, that they may behold My glory which You have given Me; for You loved Me before the foundation of the world. [25] O righteous Father! The world has not known You, but I have known You; and these have known that You sent Me. [26] And I have declared to them Your name, and will declare it, that the love with which You loved Me may be in them, and I in them."

---

7. Jesus extended the scope of His prayer to include "those who will believe in Me" (verse 20). What especially did Jesus ask the Father to give to these believers (see verses 21–23)?

_____

_____

_____

_____

_____

8. Jesus had said, "I and My Father are one" (John 10:30). What do Jesus' words say about His role in revealing the character of God to the world (see 17:24–26)?

_____

_____

_____

_____

_____

_____

REVIEWING THE STORY

In the narrative of John's Gospel, Jesus had one last opportunity to prepare His disciples for what would soon happen to Him. He not only warned them about difficulties and persecution but also comforted them with the news of the Holy Spirit's arrival and the assurance their relationship with Him would continue. Then Jesus did the most loving and productive thing that He could do for them: He *prayed*. He prayed for Himself, He prayed for them, and He prayed for those who would come to know Him through the disciples' ministry.

9. What did Jesus want the disciples to understand before His enemies came to arrest Him (see John 16:1–5)?

_____

_____

_____

_____

_____

_____

10. The disciples were used to offering daily prayers to God. What authority did Jesus now give to them if they made their requests in His name (see John 16:23–25)?

_____

_____

_____

_____

_____

_____

11. Why did Jesus say the world would hate His disciples? What did He ask God to do for them even as they remained in the world (see John 17:14–16)?

_____

_____

_____

_____

_____

_____

12. Jesus prayed that those who would come to know Him through the work of His disciples would be one (see John 17:20–23). How does unity among believers inspire others to believe the truth about Jesus?

_____

_____

_____

_____

_____

_____

APPLYING THE MESSAGE

13. What stands out to you when you read Jesus' prayers for Himself, for His disciples, and for all believers? How will they influence the way you pray to your heavenly Father?

_____

_____

_____

_____

_____

14. If you trusted in Jesus as your Savior, you are counted among the believers for whom Jesus prayed in John 17:20–26. How does it feel to know that Jesus made specific requests to His heavenly Father for *you*? What could one of those specific prayers for you have been?

REFLECTING ON THE MEANING

Jesus' prayer in John 17 reveals His present work on our behalf. He prayed out loud and in front of His disciples so they—and we—would know He is using all His influence with His Father for the benefit of His followers. Even now He is interceding for us to His Father. In effect, He is asking God, "On My behalf and for My sake, will You do these things for My disciples?"

Jesus wanted us to know He is going to use everything in His power to meet the needs we have in our lives. He wanted us to know we are precious to Him and will always have a special place in His heart. As He said to His heavenly Father, "I come to You, and these things I speak in the world, that they may have My joy fulfilled in themselves" (John 17:13).

We find this truth about Christ recorded in other passages in the New Testament. In Romans 8:34, Paul writes, "It is Christ . . . who is even at the right hand of God, who also makes intercession for us." The author of Hebrews states that Jesus "always lives to make intercession" for us, and that "Christ has not entered the holy places made with hands . . . but into heaven itself, now to appear in the presence of God for us" (7:25; 9:24). Jesus is *always* praying for us. What a comforting and empowering thought!

JOURNALING YOUR RESPONSE

What is the top request you would like Jesus to take to His heavenly Father on your behalf?

INDIGNITIES AND INJUSTICE

John 18:1–40

GETTING STARTED

If you had been one of Jesus' disciples, where do you think you would have been during His arrest and trial? What emotions do you think you would have been experiencing?

_____

_____

_____

_____

_____

_____

_____

_____

_____

SETTING THE STAGE

The way to the cross for Jesus officially began in the Garden of Gethsemane. After praying for His disciples (and for us) in the upper room, He traveled to the small garden located on the Mount of Olives, and there prepared for what was to come by praying with such intent that "His sweat became like great drops of blood falling down to the ground" (Luke 22:44).

In just a few hours, He would be betrayed by Judas Iscariot and arrested. It would be during the arrest that Peter, in trying to defend Jesus, cut off a man's ear. But during the trial that followed, three times Peter would be recognized as one of Jesus' disciples, and three times he would deny even *knowing* Christ.

Jesus endured two separate trials. The first, the Jewish (religious) trial, began with a hearing before Annas, the father-in-law of the high priest, Caiaphas. The details of the hearing are lost, as John shifted his attention to his own experiences with Peter as they followed Jesus after His arrest. Annas then sent Jesus to Caiaphas and the Sanhedrin, who hastily assembled to give the appearance that what they were doing was legal. It wasn't. The Jewish leaders had no authority to execute a prisoner. They needed Pilate, the Roman governor, to issue that order. So they sent Jesus to him for a second trial as the Roman (secular) authority in the region.

Each of the Gospels report that Pilate could find no fault in Jesus. John's Gospel contains the most extensive dialogue between Jesus and Pilate. But at the end, the result was the same in each account. Pilate offered to release Jesus as part of a Passover tradition, but the fervent Jewish crowd demanded that he release a criminal named Barabbas instead.

With this, the Jewish leaders received the verdict they had desired from Pilate, and the events would move quickly toward Jesus' execution on the cross.

EXPLORING THE TEXT

Betrayal and Arrest in Gethsemane (John 18:1–11)

---

¹ When Jesus had spoken these words, He went out with His disciples over the Brook Kidron, where there was a garden, which He and His disciples entered. ² And Judas, who betrayed Him, also knew the place; for Jesus often met there with His disciples. ³ Then Judas,

having received a detachment of troops, and officers from the chief priests and Pharisees, came there with lanterns, torches, and weapons. ⁴ Jesus therefore, knowing all things that would come upon Him, went forward and said to them, "Whom are you seeking?"

⁵ They answered Him, "Jesus of Nazareth."

Jesus said to them, "I am He." And Judas, who betrayed Him, also stood with them. ⁶ Now when He said to them, "I am He," they drew back and fell to the ground.

⁷ Then He asked them again, "Whom are you seeking?"

And they said, "Jesus of Nazareth."

⁸ Jesus answered, "I have told you that I am He. Therefore, if you seek Me, let these go their way," ⁹ that the saying might be fulfilled which He spoke, "Of those whom You gave Me I have lost none."

¹⁰ Then Simon Peter, having a sword, drew it and struck the high priest's servant, and cut off his right ear. The servant's name was Malchus.

¹¹ So Jesus said to Peter, "Put your sword into the sheath. Shall I not drink the cup which My Father has given Me?"

---

1. How did the detachment of troops accompanying Judas Iscariot react when Jesus first identified Himself? What do you think caused this reaction (see verses 3–6)?

2. How did Jesus show concern for His disciples' well-being one last time before He was arrested (see verse 8)?

_____

_____

_____

_____

_____

_____

_____

_____

_____

_____

Peter Denies Jesus (John 18:12–18)

¹² Then the detachment of troops and the captain and the officers of the Jews arrested Jesus and bound Him. ¹³ And they led Him away to Annas first, for he was the father-in-law of Caiaphas who was high priest that year. ¹⁴ Now it was Caiaphas who advised the Jews that it was expedient that one man should die for the people.

¹⁵ And Simon Peter followed Jesus, and so did another disciple. Now that disciple was known to the high priest, and went with Jesus into the courtyard of the high priest. ¹⁶ But Peter stood at the door outside. Then the other disciple, who was known to the high priest, went out and spoke to her who kept the door, and brought Peter in. ¹⁷ Then the servant girl who kept the door said to Peter, "You are not also one of this Man's disciples, are you?"

He said, "I am not."

¹⁸ Now the servants and officers who had made a fire of coals stood there, for it was cold, and they warmed themselves. And Peter stood with them and warmed himself.

3. Caiaphas believed Jesus' popularity posed a threat to Israel and feared the Roman authorities would tighten their grip on the nation if they sensed radicalism was increasing. How do you think that affected his feelings about Jesus' guilt (see verses 12–14)?

4. The "other disciple" who joined Peter in following Jesus to His trial was likely John, the author of the Gospel. How would you describe their actions that night? Do you think they were courageous, cowardly, concerned, or confused (see verses 15–17)? Explain.

Jesus Questioned by the High Priest (John 18:19–27)

19 The high priest then asked Jesus about His disciples and His doctrine.

20 Jesus answered him, "I spoke openly to the world. I always taught in synagogues and in the temple, where the Jews always meet, and in secret I have said nothing. 21 Why do you ask Me? Ask those who have heard Me what I said to them. Indeed they know what I said."

22 And when He had said these things, one of the officers who stood by struck Jesus with the palm of his hand, saying, "Do You answer the high priest like that?"

²³ Jesus answered him, "If I have spoken evil, bear witness of the evil; but if well, why do you strike Me?"

²⁴ Then Annas sent Him bound to Caiaphas the high priest.

²⁵ Now Simon Peter stood and warmed himself. Therefore they said to him, "You are not also one of His disciples, are you?"

He denied it and said, "I am not!"

²⁶ One of the servants of the high priest, a relative of him whose ear Peter cut off, said, "Did I not see you in the garden with Him?"

²⁷ Peter then denied again; and immediately a rooster crowed.

---

5. Why do you think Jesus answered Annas in the manner He did (see verses 20–23)?

_____

_____

_____

_____

_____

_____

_____

6. Just a few hours before, Peter was ready to fight for Jesus and die for Him. What do you think changed in Peter while he was in the courtyard (see verses 25–27)?

_____

_____

_____

_____

_____

_____

_____

_____

Jesus Questioned by Pilate (John 18:28–40)

[28] Then they led Jesus from Caiaphas to the Praetorium, and it was early morning. But they themselves did not go into the Praetorium, lest they should be defiled, but that they might eat the Passover. [29] Pilate then went out to them and said, "What accusation do you bring against this Man?"

[30] They answered and said to him, "If He were not an evildoer, we would not have delivered Him up to you."

[31] Then Pilate said to them, "You take Him and judge Him according to your law."

Therefore the Jews said to him, "It is not lawful for us to put anyone to death," [32] that the saying of Jesus might be fulfilled which He spoke, signifying by what death He would die.

[33] Then Pilate entered the Praetorium again, called Jesus, and said to Him, "Are You the King of the Jews?"

[34] Jesus answered him, "Are you speaking for yourself about this, or did others tell you this concerning Me?"

[35] Pilate answered, "Am I a Jew? Your own nation and the chief priests have delivered You to me. What have You done?"

[36] Jesus answered, "My kingdom is not of this world. If My kingdom were of this world, My servants would fight, so that I should not be delivered to the Jews; but now My kingdom is not from here."

[37] Pilate therefore said to Him, "Are You a king then?"

Jesus answered, "You say rightly that I am a king. For this cause I was born, and for this cause I have come into the world, that I should bear witness to the truth. Everyone who is of the truth hears My voice."

[38] Pilate said to Him, "What is truth?" And when he had said this, he went out again to the Jews, and said to them, "I find no fault in Him at all.

[39] "But you have a custom that I should release someone to you at the Passover. Do you therefore want me to release to you the King of the Jews?"

⁴⁰ Then they all cried again, saying, "Not this Man, but Barabbas!" Now Barabbas was a robber.

---

7. How did the Jewish leaders answer Pilate when he asked them about the charges against Jesus? Why do you think they responded that way (see verses 30–32)?

_____

_____

_____

_____

_____

_____

8. How did Jesus answer when Pilate asked if He were the King of the Jews (see verses 33–37)?

_____

_____

_____

_____

_____

_____

_____

REVIEWING THE STORY

A night that would be filled with indignities and injustice began with Jesus' betrayer, Judas Iscariot, invading Jesus' prayer sanctuary in the Garden of Gethsemane, accompanied by armed troops to arrest the Savior. Jesus was bound and taken to Annas, where He was illegally questioned and assaulted. He was then taken to the Roman governor, Pilate, who could find no fault with Him but sentenced Him to death anyway to appease the Jewish leaders. Meanwhile, Peter, who hours earlier had vowed to die with Jesus, three times denied even knowing Him.

9. Read Matthew 26:1–5. Why do you think such a large and heavily armed contingent went with Judas Iscariot to arrest Jesus (see John 18:3)?

_____

_____

_____

_____

_____

_____

_____

_____

10. John notes the "other disciple" with Peter (likely John himself) was known to the high priest. This disciple was allowed entrance into the courtyard, and when he spoke to the woman at the door, Peter was also allowed to enter. What would be the repercussions of this simple act of kindness (see John 18:16–17, 25–27)?

_____

_____

_____

_____

_____

_____

_____

11. How would you describe Jesus' demeanor when He appeared before Annas—who was a powerful man among the religious elite? How does John show that Jesus was really the one in control throughout His trials (see John 18:20–23)?

12. How did Pilate attempt to determine if Jesus was guilty of the claims the Jewish leaders had brought against Him? What was his ultimate conclusion (see John 18:33–38)?

APPLYING THE MESSAGE

13. Jesus retreated to the Garden of Gethsemane to seek His heavenly Father in prayer when He was feeling overwhelmed. What do you learn from His example? Where do you go to pray when circumstances threaten to overpower you?

14. Read Hebrews 4:15. Why is Jesus the perfect person to talk to when you are feeling overwhelmed, when you have been betrayed by a friend, when you seem to be surrounded by enemies, or when you are facing extremely difficult circumstances?

REFLECTING ON THE MEANING

There are two lessons we must not miss when we examine the trials of Jesus. For in these trials we see a cross section of humanity today—especially in their responses to the Lord.

In Jesus' enemies, we see *the weakness of wickedness*. According to Jewish law, an accused person was not required to testify against himself. But this was exactly what Annas had in mind when he required Jesus to appear before him under the cover of night. We also see the pious and sanctimonious nature of the Jewish leaders' sin when they take precautions not to violate Jewish law even as they prepare to crucify the Son of God. As John writes, "They led Jesus from Caiaphas to the Praetorium, and it was early morning. But they themselves did not go into the Praetorium, lest they should be defiled" (18:28).

In Pilate we see *the wickedness of weakness*. Pilate demonstrated his weakness first in his refusal to face the issue. He question the Jewish leaders as to why they had brought Jesus to him. Luke tells us that when Pilate learned Jesus was from Galilee, he tried to pass the matter off to Herod, who held jurisdiction over that region. When Herod proved to be no help, Pilate appealed to a Jewish custom of releasing a prisoner at Passover. He hoped the crowd would allow him to release Jesus, but instead they called for the release of the criminal Barabbas.

Pilate also demonstrated his weakness in consciously making the *wrong* decision. He said he could find no fault with Jesus, yet ultimately he gave in to the pressures of the crowd and agreed to hand over Jesus to be crucified. He even dismissed an appeal from his wife to "have nothing to do with that just Man, for I have suffered many things in a dream because of Him" (Matthew 27:19). The sign Pilate had placed on Jesus' cross, "Jesus of Nazareth, the King of the Jews," suggests that he may have well recognized the truth.

JOURNALING YOUR RESPONSE

How has God helped you to not give in to the pressures of other people when it comes to making the right decision?

THE HILL OF GOLGOTHA

John 19:1–42

GETTING STARTED

When were some times that your desire to please other people proved to be more important to you than doing something you knew was right? What happened as a result?

_____

_____

_____

_____

_____

_____

_____

_____

_____

_____

_____

SETTING THE STAGE

Mary, the mother of Jesus, was a godly woman of great personal strength. There was a reason God chose her to be the vehicle through which His own Son, Jesus, would be born.

Mary was found to be "with child" when she was betrothed to Joseph. The child Jesus that she carried in her womb was conceived by the Holy Spirit. Mary was not even in her twenties when this happened—she was likely between the ages of sixteen and eighteen. Just try to imagine the overwhelming issues she would have faced when the angel announced she would be the mother of our Lord. Many of the things Mary pondered in her heart during Jesus' life came to fruition in the events recorded in John 19:25–27, which presents Jesus hanging on the cross. Yet even in the midst of all His suffering, He recognized His mother.

In just three short verses of Scripture, Jesus magnified the role of motherhood for all of eternity. In the last moments of His agony on the cross, He turned from His own pain and saw His mother. Conceived of the Holy Spirit, nurtured in her womb, and loved throughout His life, He reached out to her in His dying moments.

Standing around the cross that day were other women who followed Jesus. By comparing the Gospel accounts, we can identify at least three: (1) Mary Magdalene, the woman from whom Jesus had cast out seven demons; (2) Mary, the mother of James and Joses (referred to as the wife of Clopas in John's Gospel); and (3) Salome (referred to as the mother of James and John in Matthew's Gospel). Only John mentions the presence of Jesus' mother. Only John, alone among the disciples, was there to witness Jesus' death on the cross.

When Jesus finished His instruction to Mary and to John, He died the awful death of crucifixion. The Bible states that when they left the hill of Golgotha, they went to their own homes, and John took Mary to his home in obedience to the Lord's instruction.

EXPLORING THE TEXT

Jesus Sentenced to Be Crucified (John 19:1–12)

---

[1] So then Pilate took Jesus and scourged Him. [2] And the soldiers twisted a crown of thorns and put it on His head, and they put on

Him a purple robe. ³ Then they said, "Hail, King of the Jews!" And they struck Him with their hands.

⁴ Pilate then went out again, and said to them, "Behold, I am bringing Him out to you, that you may know that I find no fault in Him."

⁵ Then Jesus came out, wearing the crown of thorns and the purple robe. And Pilate said to them, "Behold the Man!"

⁶ Therefore, when the chief priests and officers saw Him, they cried out, saying, "Crucify Him, crucify Him!"

Pilate said to them, "You take Him and crucify Him, for I find no fault in Him."

⁷ The Jews answered him, "We have a law, and according to our law He ought to die, because He made Himself the Son of God."

⁸ Therefore, when Pilate heard that saying, he was the more afraid, ⁹ and went again into the Praetorium, and said to Jesus, "Where are You from?" But Jesus gave him no answer.

¹⁰ Then Pilate said to Him, "Are You not speaking to me? Do You not know that I have power to crucify You, and power to release You?"

¹¹ Jesus answered, "You could have no power at all against Me unless it had been given you from above. Therefore the one who delivered Me to you has the greater sin."

¹² From then on Pilate sought to release Him, but the Jews cried out, saying, "If you let this Man go, you are not Caesar's friend. Whoever makes himself a king speaks against Caesar."

---

1. It was Pilate's responsibility to respect and, when necessary, enforce the religious law of the Jewish people. How did the Jewish leaders use this to persuade Pilate (see verses 6–9)?

....

....

....

....

2. What was Pilate's mistaken idea about the power he wielded (see verses 10–11)?

_____

_____

_____

_____

_____

_____

_____

_____

_____

_____

The King on a Cross (John 19:13–22)

¹³ When Pilate therefore heard that saying, he brought Jesus out and sat down in the judgment seat in a place that is called The Pavement, but in Hebrew, Gabbatha. ¹⁴ Now it was the Preparation Day of the Passover, and about the sixth hour. And he said to the Jews, "Behold your King!"

¹⁵ But they cried out, "Away with Him, away with Him! Crucify Him!"

Pilate said to them, "Shall I crucify your King?"

The chief priests answered, "We have no king but Caesar!"

¹⁶ Then he delivered Him to them to be crucified. Then they took Jesus and led Him away.

¹⁷ And He, bearing His cross, went out to a place called the Place of a Skull, which is called in Hebrew, Golgotha, ¹⁸ where they crucified Him, and two others with Him, one on either side, and Jesus in the center. ¹⁹ Now Pilate wrote a title and put it on the cross. And the writing was:

JESUS OF NAZARETH, THE KING OF THE JEWS.

²⁰ Then many of the Jews read this title, for the place where Jesus was crucified was near the city; and it was written in Hebrew, Greek, and Latin.

²¹ Therefore the chief priests of the Jews said to Pilate, "Do not write, 'The King of the Jews,' but, 'He said, "I am the King of the Jews." ' "

²² Pilate answered, "What I have written, I have written."

---

3. The Jewish people hated the Romans and yearned to be free from their control. What hypocritical words did they speak to convince Pilate to crucify Jesus (see verses 15–16)?

_____

_____

_____

_____

_____

4. Pilate intended the sign he wrote to serve as an insult and mockery of Christ. But what objection did the Jewish leaders raise about it (see verses 19–22)?

_____

_____

_____

_____

_____

_____

It Is Finished (John 19:23–30)

²³ Then the soldiers, when they had crucified Jesus, took His garments and made four parts, to each soldier a part, and also the tunic. Now the tunic was without seam, woven from the top in one piece. ²⁴ They said therefore among themselves, "Let us not tear it, but cast lots for it, whose it shall be," that the Scripture might be fulfilled which says:

"They divided My garments among them,
And for My clothing they cast lots."

Therefore the soldiers did these things.

²⁵ Now there stood by the cross of Jesus His mother, and His mother's sister, Mary the wife of Clopas, and Mary Magdalene. ²⁶ When Jesus therefore saw His mother, and the disciple whom He loved standing by, He said to His mother, "Woman, behold your son!" ²⁷ Then He said to the disciple, "Behold your mother!" And from that hour that disciple took her to his own home.

²⁸ After this, Jesus, knowing that all things were now accomplished, that the Scripture might be fulfilled, said, "I thirst!" ²⁹ Now a vessel full of sour wine was sitting there; and they filled a sponge with sour wine, put it on hyssop, and put it to His mouth. ³⁰ So when Jesus had received the sour wine, He said, "It is finished!" And bowing His head, He gave up His spirit.

---

5. Read Psalm 22:18. How did the Roman soldiers at Jesus' crucifixion fulfill a prophecy without even realizing it (see John 19:23–24)?

_____

_____

_____

_____

6. What do you think Jesus was referring to when He said, *"It* is finished" (verse 30)?

_____

_____

_____

_____

_____

_____

Jesus' Side Is Pierced (John 19:31–42)

³¹ Therefore, because it was the Preparation Day, that the bodies should not remain on the cross on the Sabbath (for that Sabbath was a high day), the Jews asked Pilate that their legs might be broken, and that they might be taken away. ³² Then the soldiers came and broke the legs of the first and of the other who was crucified with Him. ³³ But when they came to Jesus and saw that He was already dead, they did not break His legs. ³⁴ But one of the soldiers pierced His side with a spear, and immediately blood and water came out. ³⁵ And he who has seen has testified, and his testimony is true; and he knows that he is telling the truth, so that you may believe. ³⁶ For these things were done that the Scripture should be fulfilled, "Not one of His bones shall be broken." ³⁷ And again another Scripture says, "They shall look on Him whom they pierced."

³⁸ After this, Joseph of Arimathea, being a disciple of Jesus, but secretly, for fear of the Jews, asked Pilate that he might take away the body of Jesus; and Pilate gave him permission. So he came and took the body of Jesus. ³⁹ And Nicodemus, who at first came to Jesus by night, also came, bringing a mixture of myrrh and aloes, about a hundred pounds. ⁴⁰ Then they took the body of Jesus, and bound it in strips of linen with the spices, as the custom of the Jews is to bury. ⁴¹ Now in the place where He was crucified there was a garden, and

in the garden a new tomb in which no one had yet been laid. ⁴² So there they laid Jesus, because of the Jews' Preparation Day, for the tomb was nearby.

---

7. What measures did the soldiers take to make sure Jesus was truly dead? Why does John stress this particular point (see verses 32–35)?

_____

_____

_____

_____

8. Joseph of Arimathea and Nicodemus were likely two of the richest men in Jerusalem. Why do you think they were so secretive about being disciples of Jesus (see verses 38–39)?

_____

_____

_____

_____

REVIEWING THE STORY

One of Jesus' most extraordinary feats was maintaining His focus on God's plan of salvation and accomplishing everything He needed to do under the most excruciating circumstances. He endured the torture and the mocking of the Roman soldiers. He made no effort to defend Himself against false accusations. With His wrists and feet nailed to a wooden cross, and with soldiers gambling for His only possessions, He ensured that His mother would be cared for after His death. He also ensured that all of the remaining prophecies concerning the Messiah would be fulfilled . . . proving once and for all that He is the Son of God.

9. What ultimately led Pilate to sentence Jesus to death (see John 19:4–8)?

10. A basic belief among the people of Israel was that God alone was their king (see Judges 8:23). How did the religious leaders reveal just how far they had separated themselves from God when they cried for Pilate to crucify Jesus (see John 19:14–15)?

11. Why do you think John makes a point of saying that Jesus "gave up His spirit" instead of simply saying that He died? How does this final act reveal Jesus' ultimate submission to the will of His Father (see John 19:30)?

12. Usually, the Roman executioners would break the legs of those who were crucified to speed up their deaths. This didn't happen to Jesus, however, because He was already dead (see John 19:31–33). How did this fulfill the prophecy found in Psalm 34:20?

_____

_____

_____

_____

_____

_____

_____

_____

_____

APPLYING THE MESSAGE

13. If someone asked you why Jesus had to die on the cross, what would you say?

_____

_____

_____

_____

_____

_____

_____

_____

_____

14. What should be a Christian's attitude toward Jesus' crucifixion? Explain.

_____

_____

_____

_____

_____

REFLECTING ON THE MEANING

Four events occurred at Jesus' crucifixion that often go unnoticed. The first event is that *a prophecy was fulfilled*. When Joseph and Mary took the baby Jesus to the temple to be dedicated, an elderly man named Simeon prophesied that because of Jesus, the destiny of many in Israel would be determined. He also prophesied that because of Jesus, a sword would pierce Mary's soul (see Luke 2:34–35). The pain of watching her Son suffer on the cross surely pierced Mary's soul like a sword.

The second event is that *a prodigal was restored*. According to Matthew, on the night of Jesus' arrest, His disciples all "forsook Him and fled" (26:56). When the Shepherd was struck down, the sheep were scattered. The disciples of Jesus wanted nothing to do with Him as He was being led to the hill of Golgotha. Yet one of them came back. John, the disciple whom Jesus loved, stood at the foot of Jesus' cross, loyal to the end.

The third event is that *a principle was reinforced*. The cornerstone of Jewish family life was God's command to "honor your father and your mother" (Exodus 20:12). When parents reached a certain age, a loving son honored them by caring for them or arranging for their care. In His dying moment, Jesus honored His mother, Mary (His earthly father Joseph had died years earlier), by entrusting her care to His beloved disciple John.

The fourth event is that *a priority was recognized*. Mary had other sons, who were Jesus' half-brothers. Why didn't Jesus leave her in the care of one of them? The reason is certainly because His brothers at the time did not believe He was the Messiah. They weren't part of His spiritual family. As Jesus said in Matthew 12:50, "For whoever does the will of My father in heaven is My brother and sister and mother."

JOURNALING YOUR RESPONSE

What does Jesus' death mean for your life? What have you received as a result of His sacrifice?

FOUR REMARKABLE ENCOUNTERS

John 20:1–21:25

GETTING STARTED

What is your favorite fairytale ending, whether in a book, movie, or television show? What makes it so good?

SETTING THE STAGE

Jesus of Nazareth had been crucified, and the city of Jerusalem reverberated with the aftershocks. Everyone had an opinion about the late prophet from Galilee. His death was a relief to many. His presence in the temple city had disrupted their lives. With His passing, they could get back to their previous routines.

For others, the death of Jesus meant mourning. Grief filled their hearts . . . much like the despair that comes from the death of a national hero. They had not only believed in Him but had also loved Him. They had hoped and trusted that He was the deliverer who would lift the bondage of the Romans from their shoulders. But the object of their hopes had instead been lifted upon a cross, killed by the very Roman Empire that He was expected to conquer. His body had been placed in a tomb. As far as the mourners knew, there was no bringing Him back. Their hope was gone. They were devastated and in shock.

But then, on the third day after His crucifixion, strange rumors began to circulate. People were saying that Jesus' body was not where it had been placed in the tomb of Joseph of Arimathea. Many were saying Christ had risen from the dead. Reports started circling of people seeing Him. People were saying He had appeared to Mary Magdalene early on Sunday, and then, later, to other women who came to the tomb. Soon after, He had revealed Himself to ten disciples assembled in an upper room.

The resurrection of Jesus Christ is one of the best-documented stories in all history. But it is also a human story. It happened as it did to those who were there in Jerusalem at that time.

EXPLORING THE TEXT

The Empty Tomb (John 20:1–18)

¹ Now the first day of the week Mary Magdalene went to the tomb early, while it was still dark, and saw that the stone had been taken

away from the tomb. [2] Then she ran and came to Simon Peter, and to the other disciple, whom Jesus loved, and said to them, "They have taken away the Lord out of the tomb, and we do not know where they have laid Him."

[3] Peter therefore went out, and the other disciple, and were going to the tomb. [4] So they both ran together, and the other disciple outran Peter and came to the tomb first. [5] And he, stooping down and looking in, saw the linen cloths lying there; yet he did not go in. [6] Then Simon Peter came, following him, and went into the tomb; and he saw the linen cloths lying there, [7] and the handkerchief that had been around His head, not lying with the linen cloths, but folded together in a place by itself. [8] Then the other disciple, who came to the tomb first, went in also; and he saw and believed. [9] For as yet they did not know the Scripture, that He must rise again from the dead. [10] Then the disciples went away again to their own homes.

[11] But Mary stood outside by the tomb weeping, and as she wept she stooped down and looked into the tomb. [12] And she saw two angels in white sitting, one at the head and the other at the feet, where the body of Jesus had lain. [13] Then they said to her, "Woman, why are you weeping?"

She said to them, "Because they have taken away my Lord, and I do not know where they have laid Him."

[14] Now when she had said this, she turned around and saw Jesus standing there, and did not know that it was Jesus. [15] Jesus said to her, "Woman, why are you weeping? Whom are you seeking?"

She, supposing Him to be the gardener, said to Him, "Sir, if You have carried Him away, tell me where You have laid Him, and I will take Him away."

[16] Jesus said to her, "Mary!"

She turned and said to Him, "Rabboni!" (which is to say, Teacher).

[17] Jesus said to her, "Do not cling to Me, for I have not yet ascended to My Father; but go to My brethren and say to them,

'I am ascending to My Father and your Father, and to My God and your God.' "

¹⁸ Mary Magdalene came and told the disciples that she had seen the Lord, and that He had spoken these things to her.

---

1. Jesus' burial had been hurried, and now Mary Magdalene (and other women) were returning to the tomb to prepare the body. What did she discover when she arrived? How did Peter and "the other disciple" respond to Mary's news (see verses 1–4)?

_____

_____

_____

_____

_____

2. How did Mary respond to the angels' question? Why do you think she did not recognize Jesus until He said her name (see verses 12–16)?

_____

_____

_____

_____

Jesus Appears to His Disciples (John 20:19–31)

¹⁹ Then, the same day at evening, being the first day of the week, when the doors were shut where the disciples were assembled, for fear of the Jews, Jesus came and stood in the midst, and said to them, "Peace be with you." ²⁰ When He had said this, He showed them His hands and His side. Then the disciples were glad when they saw the Lord.

²¹ So Jesus said to them again, "Peace to you! As the Father has sent Me, I also send you." ²² And when He had said this, He breathed on them, and said to them, "Receive the Holy Spirit. ²³ If you forgive the sins of any, they are forgiven them; if you retain the sins of any, they are retained."

²⁴ Now Thomas, called the Twin, one of the twelve, was not with them when Jesus came. ²⁵ The other disciples therefore said to him, "We have seen the Lord."

So he said to them, "Unless I see in His hands the print of the nails, and put my finger into the print of the nails, and put my hand into His side, I will not believe."

²⁶ And after eight days His disciples were again inside, and Thomas with them. Jesus came, the doors being shut, and stood in the midst, and said, "Peace to you!" ²⁷ Then He said to Thomas, "Reach your finger here, and look at My hands; and reach your hand here, and put it into My side. Do not be unbelieving, but believing."

²⁸ And Thomas answered and said to Him, "My Lord and my God!"

²⁹ Jesus said to him, "Thomas, because you have seen Me, you have believed. Blessed are those who have not seen and yet have believed."

³⁰ And truly Jesus did many other signs in the presence of His disciples, which are not written in this book; ³¹ but these are written that you may believe that Jesus is the Christ, the Son of God, and that believing you may have life in His name.

---

3. Thomas was not with the other disciples when Jesus appeared to them. How did Jesus help Thomas overcome his doubts and strengthen his faith (see verses 24–29)?

4. John writes that Jesus performed "many other signs" in the presence of His disciples. What was John's criteria for choosing which ones to include in his Gospel (see verses 30–31)?

_____

_____

_____

_____

_____

_____

Breakfast by the Sea (John 21:1–13)

¹ After these things Jesus showed Himself again to the disciples at the Sea of Tiberias, and in this way He showed Himself: ² Simon Peter, Thomas called the Twin, Nathanael of Cana in Galilee, the sons of Zebedee, and two others of His disciples were together. ³ Simon Peter said to them, "I am going fishing."

They said to him, "We are going with you also." They went out and immediately got into the boat, and that night they caught nothing. ⁴ But when the morning had now come, Jesus stood on the shore; yet the disciples did not know that it was Jesus. ⁵ Then Jesus said to them, "Children, have you any food?"

They answered Him, "No."

⁶ And He said to them, "Cast the net on the right side of the boat, and you will find some." So they cast, and now they were not able to draw it in because of the multitude of fish.

⁷ Therefore that disciple whom Jesus loved said to Peter, "It is the Lord!" Now when Simon Peter heard that it was the Lord, he put on his outer garment (for he had removed it), and plunged into the sea. ⁸ But the other disciples came in the little boat (for they were not far from land, but about two hundred cubits), dragging the net with fish. ⁹ Then, as soon as they had come to land, they saw a fire

of coals there, and fish laid on it, and bread. ¹⁰ Jesus said to them, "Bring some of the fish which you have just caught."

¹¹ Simon Peter went up and dragged the net to land, full of large fish, one hundred and fifty-three; and although there were so many, the net was not broken. ¹² Jesus said to them, "Come and eat breakfast." Yet none of the disciples dared ask Him, "Who are You?"—knowing that it was the Lord. ¹³ Jesus then came and took the bread and gave it to them, and likewise the fish.

5. Read Luke 5:1–11. How was Jesus' appearance to Peter and the others at the Sea of Tiberias (Galilee) similar to His first encounter with them? How was it different (see John 21:1–6)?

6. How did Peter respond when he realized Jesus was on the shore? What do you imagine he was thinking when he saw Jesus had prepared a breakfast for them (see verses 7–10)?

Jesus Reinstates Peter (John 21:15–25)

¹⁵ So when they had eaten breakfast, Jesus said to Simon Peter, "Simon, son of Jonah, do you love Me more than these?"

He said to Him, "Yes, Lord; You know that I love You."

He said to him, "Feed My lambs."

[16] He said to him again a second time, "Simon, son of Jonah, do you love Me?"

He said to Him, "Yes, Lord; You know that I love You."

He said to him, "Tend My sheep."

[17] He said to him the third time, "Simon, son of Jonah, do you love Me?" Peter was grieved because He said to him the third time, "Do you love Me?"

And he said to Him, "Lord, You know all things; You know that I love You."

Jesus said to him, "Feed My sheep. [18] Most assuredly, I say to you, when you were younger, you girded yourself and walked where you wished; but when you are old, you will stretch out your hands, and another will gird you and carry you where you do not wish." [19] This He spoke, signifying by what death he would glorify God. And when He had spoken this, He said to him, "Follow Me."

[20] Then Peter, turning around, saw the disciple whom Jesus loved following, who also had leaned on His breast at the supper, and said, "Lord, who is the one who betrays You?" [21] Peter, seeing him, said to Jesus, "But Lord, what about this man?"

[22] Jesus said to him, "If I will that he remain till I come, what is that to you? You follow Me."

[23] Then this saying went out among the brethren that this disciple would not die. Yet Jesus did not say to him that he would not die, but, "If I will that he remain till I come, what is that to you?"

[24] This is the disciple who testifies of these things, and wrote these things; and we know that his testimony is true.

[25] And there are also many other things that Jesus did, which if they were written one by one, I suppose that even the world itself could not contain the books that would be written. Amen.

7. Review John 18:15–25. Why do you think Jesus specifically asked Peter *three* times if he loved Him (see John 21:15–17)?

_____

_____

_____

_____

_____

8. According to church history, Peter was crucified for spreading the good news of Christ. What hints does Christ give as to the manner in which Peter would die (see verses 18–19)?

_____

_____

_____

_____

REVIEWING THE STORY

John relates in the final two chapters of his Gospel how the resurrected Jesus comforted, prepared, encouraged, and restored His followers. He first appeared to Mary Magdalene outside the tomb to relieve her sadness and give her good news to deliver to the disciples. He later appeared to several of His disciples and breathed His Spirit into them to ready them for the work that would soon begin. When Thomas refused to believe what the others had seen, Jesus appeared again to him. He encouraged Thomas to examine His wounds to allay the disciple's doubts. Finally, Jesus restored fellowship with Peter after his three denials.

9. What did Peter and John ("the other disciple") see when they arrived at the tomb of Christ? What is it that John "believed" when he witnessed the scene (see John 20:3–10)?

_____

_____

_____

_____

10. The future work of the disciples would be extremely difficult and extremely dangerous. What did Jesus do to prepare them for it (see John 20:21–23)?

_____

_____

_____

_____

11. Why do you think Peter and the other disciples went back to fishing after they had seen the resurrected Jesus (see John 21:1–5)?

_____

_____

_____

12. Jesus referred to Himself as a good shepherd, and everyone who followed Him was part of His flock (see John 10:1–30). What assignments did Jesus give Peter in His three-part question-and-instruction session that related to His flock (see John 21:15–17)?

_____

_____

_____

APPLYING THE MESSAGE

13. What evidence do you find in John 20–21 to offer someone who refuses to believe that Jesus rose from the dead?

_____

_____

_____

_____

14. In what ways (or areas) are you relying on yourself more than you are relying on God as you seek to live as a disciple of Christ?

_____

_____

_____

_____

REFLECTING ON THE MEANING

"Feed my lambs." "Tend my sheep." "Feed my sheep." Those were the three commands Jesus gave Peter (see John 21:15–17). Although there are slight variations in the wording, all three are calls to *edification*. In the Greek, the words that combine to form *edification* mean "to build" and "house." Jesus wasn't calling Peter to build a house, but He was calling Peter to build up disciples. Jesus issues the same calling to you as well.

As you seek to build up disciples, there are a few "principles of edification" you need to understand. The first is that *edification is not about you but about others*. Often, this will mean sacrificing your own comfort, freedom, and preferences to seek the best interests of others.

The second principle is that *edification is not about what you profess but about what you pursue*. Building up others does not come naturally to most people. If you want to edify the people in your world, you must work to overcome your natural instincts to tear them down.

The third principle is that *edification is not about how much you know but about how much you care*. In 1 Corinthians 8:1, Paul states, "Knowledge puffs up, but love edifies." Without the love of God, all the knowledge in the world is virtually useless.

The fourth principle is that *edification is not about your gifts but about your goals*. Your spiritual gifts have value only when you use them to benefit others. Make sure that when you exercise your gifts, it's with a specific goal in mind . . . building up others.

The fifth principle is that *edification is not about your wisdom but about God's Word*. You can't rely on your own knowledge or experience. The way to edify others is to immerse yourself in God's Word and let God's wisdom flow through you.

JOURNALING YOUR RESPONSE

When you think of an edifying person, who comes to mind? What qualities do you appreciate in that person? How can you incorporate those qualities into your own life?

LEADER'S GUIDE

Thank you for choosing to lead your group through this study from Dr. David Jeremiah on *The Gospel of John*. Being a group leader has its own rewards, and it is our prayer that your walk with the Lord will deepen through this experience. During the twelve lessons in this study, you and your group will read selected passages from John, explore key themes in the Gospel based on teachings from Dr. Jeremiah, and review questions that will encourage group discussion. There are multiple components in this section that can help you structure your lessons and discussion time, so please be sure to read and consider each one.

BEFORE YOU BEGIN

Before your first meeting, make sure you and your group are well-versed with the content of the lesson. Group members should have their own copy of *The Gospel of John* study guide prior to the first meeting so they can follow along and record their answers, thoughts, and insights. After the first week, you may wish to assign the study guide lesson as homework prior to the group meeting and then use the meeting time to discuss the content in the lesson.

To ensure everyone has a chance to participate in the discussion, the ideal size for a group is around eight to ten people. If there are more than ten people, break up the bigger group into smaller subgroups. Make sure the members are committed to participating each week, as this will help create stability and help you better prepare the structure of the meeting.

At the beginning of each week's study, start with the opening Getting Started question to introduce the topic you will be discussing. The members should answer briefly, as the goal is just for them to have an idea of the subject in their minds as you go over the lesson. This will allow the members to become engaged and ready to interact with the rest of the group.

After reviewing the lesson, try to initiate a free-flowing discussion. Invite group members to bring questions and insights they may have discovered to the next meeting, especially if they were unsure of the meaning of some parts of the lesson. Be prepared to discuss how biblical truth applies to the world we live in today.

WEEKLY PREPARATION

As the group leader, here are a few things you can do to prepare for each meeting:

- *Be thoroughly familiar with the material in the lesson.* Make sure you understand the content of each lesson so you know how to structure the group time and are prepared to lead the group discussion.

- *Decide, ahead of time, which questions you want to discuss.* Depending on how much time you have each week, you may not be able to reflect on every question. Select specific questions that you feel will evoke the best discussion.

- *Take prayer requests.* At the end of your discussion, take prayer requests from your group members and then pray for one another.

STRUCTURING THE DISCUSSION TIME

There are several ways to structure the duration of the study. You can choose to cover each lesson individually, for a total of twelve weeks of group meetings, or you can combine two lessons together per week, for a total of six weeks of group meetings. You can also have the group members read just the selected passages of Scripture that are given in each lesson, or they can cover the entire Gospel of John. The following charts illustrates these options:

TWELVE-WEEK FORMAT

Week	Lessons Covered	Expanded Reading
1	In the Beginning	John 1:1–2:25
2	Whoever Believes in Him	John 3:1–4:54
3	The Bread of Life	John 5:1–6:71
4	Hostile Reactions	John 7:1–8:59
5	An Eye-Opening Experience	John 9:1–10:42
6	A Premature Burial	John 11:1–57
7	Treacherous Times	John 12:1–13:38
8	The True Vine	John 14:1–15:27
9	The Prayers of Jesus	John 16:1–17:26
10	Indignities and Injustice	John 18:1–40
11	The Hill of Golgotha	John 19:1–42
12	Four Remarkable Encounters	John 20:1–21:25

SIX-WEEK FORMAT

Week	Lessons Covered	Expanded Reading
1	In the Beginning / Whoever Believes in Him	John 1:1–4:54
2	The Bread of Life / Hostile Reactions	John 5:1–8:59
3	An Eye-Opening Experience / A Premature Burial	John 9:1–11:57
4	Treacherous Times / The True Vine	John 12:1–15:27
5	The Prayers of Jesus / Indignities and Injustice	John 16:1–18:40
6	The Hill of Golgotha / Four Remarkable Encounters	John 19:1–21:25

In regard to organizing your time when planning your group Bible study, the following two schedules, for sixty minutes and ninety minutes, can give you a structure for the lesson:

Section	60 Minutes	90 Minutes
Welcome: Members arrive and get settled	5 minutes	10 minutes
Getting Started Question: Prepares the group for interacting with one another	10 minutes	10 minutes
Message: Review the lesson	15 minutes	25 minutes
Discussion: Discuss questions in the lesson	25 minutes	35 minutes
Review and Prayer: Review the key points of the lesson and have a closing time of prayer	5 minutes	10 minutes

As the group leader, it is up to you to keep track of the time and keep things moving according to your schedule. If your group is having a good discussion, don't feel the need to stop and move on to the next question. Remember, the purpose is to pull together ideas and share unique insights on the lesson. Encourage everyone to participate, but don't be concerned if certain group members are more quiet. They may just be internally reflecting on the questions and need time to process their ideas before they can share them.

GROUP DYNAMICS

Leading a group study can be a rewarding experience for you and your group members—but that doesn't mean there won't be challenges. Certain members may feel uncomfortable discussing topics that they consider very personal and might be afraid of being called on. Some members might have disagreements on specific issues. To help prevent these scenarios, consider the following ground rules:

- If someone has a question that may seem off topic, suggest that it is discussed at another time, or ask the group if they are okay with addressing that topic.

- If someone asks a question you don't know the answer to, confess that you don't know and move on. If you feel comfortable, invite other group members to give their opinions or share their comments based on personal experience.
- If you feel like a couple of people are talking much more than others, direct questions to people who may not have shared yet. You could even ask the more dominating members to help draw out the quiet ones.
- When there is a disagreement, encourage the group members to process the matter in love. Invite members from opposing sides to evaluate their opinions and consider the ideas of the other members. Lead the group through Scripture that addresses the topic, and look for common ground.

When issues arise, encourage your group to think of Scripture: "Love one another" (John 13:34), "If it is possible, as much as it depends on you, live peaceably with all men" (Romans 12:18), and, "Be swift to hear, slow to speak, slow to wrath" (James 1:19).

ABOUT
Dr. David Jeremiah and Turning Point

Dr. David Jeremiah is the founder of Turning Point, a ministry committed to providing Christians with sound Bible teaching relevant to today's changing times through radio and television broadcasts, audio series, books, and live events. Dr. Jeremiah's teaching on topics such as family, prayer, worship, angels, and biblical prophecy forms the foundation of Turning Point.

David and his wife, Donna, reside in El Cajon, California, where he serves as the senior pastor of Shadow Mountain Community Church. David and Donna have four children and twelve grandchildren.

In 1982, Dr. Jeremiah brought the same solid teaching to San Diego television that he shares weekly with his congregation. Shortly thereafter, Turning Point expanded its ministry to radio. Dr. Jeremiah's inspiring messages can now be heard worldwide on radio, television, and the internet.

Because Dr. Jeremiah desires to know his listening audience, he travels nationwide holding ministry rallies and spiritual enrichment conferences that touch the hearts and lives of many people. According to Dr. Jeremiah, "At some point in time, everyone reaches a turning point; and for every person, that moment is unique, an experience to hold onto forever. There's so much changing in today's world that sometimes it's difficult to choose the right path. Turning Point offers people an understanding of God's Word and seeks to make a difference in their lives."

Dr. Jeremiah has authored numerous books, including *Escape the Coming Night* (Revelation), *The Handwriting on the Wall* (Daniel), *Overcoming Loneliness, Prayer—The Great Adventure, God in You* (Holy Spirit), *When*

Your World Falls Apart, Slaying the Giants in Your Life, My Heart's Desire, Hope for Today, Captured by Grace, Signs of Life, What in the World Is Going On?, The Coming Economic Armageddon, I Never Thought I'd See the Day!, God Loves You: He Always Has—He Always Will, Agents of the Apocalypse, Agents of Babylon, Revealing the Mysteries of Heaven, People Are Asking . . . Is This the End?, A Life Beyond Amazing, Overcomer, and *The Book of Signs.*